THE
FAMILY
EDGE

FAMILIUS

To Theresa, the North Star of our family.

Published by Familius LLC, www.familius.com

Familius books are available at special discounts for bulk purchases, whether for sales promotions or for family or corporate use. For more information, contact Familius Sales at 559-876-2170 or email orders@familius.com.

Library of Congress Cataloging-in-Publication Data
2019935083

Print ISBN 9781641701402
Ebook ISBN 9781641702034

Printed in the United States of America

Edited by Joseph Webb, Kaylee Mason, and Alison Strobel
Cover design by David Miles
Book design by Brooke Jorden

10 9 8 7 6 5 4 3 2 1

First Edition

THE
FAMILY
EDGE

How Your Biggest Competitive Advantage in Business Isn't What You've Been Taught—It's Your Family

GIBB DYER, PHD

ACKNOWLEDGMENTS

I would like to thank several people who helped me research and write this book. My research assistants Sarah Mader, Anne-Katherine Toronto, Mark Malmgren, Peter Fuller, and Luke Webster provided me with much of the data used to compare families in the United States and across the world, and they also put together an annotated bibliography of various family studies related to family capital. Adam Turville and my son, Justin Dyer, did much of the work putting the data together and doing the statistical analyses found in chapter 1. Without their help, it would have been impossible to see the impact of family capital on company start-ups and success. Our department secretarial team of Sophie Poulsen, Kesley B. Powell, and Katy Milagro Nottingham helped to produce many of the tables and figures in the book. Aaron Shelley collected most of the data regarding the family histories presented in chapter 3. I spent many hours with Aaron discussing the role family structure plays in developing family capital, which helped to sharpen my thinking. My brother Jeffrey Dyer provided me with feedback on several chapters, and Aislin Powell Dyer, my daughter-in-law and an excellent editor, helped make the book substantially more readable. (Due to the efforts of several of my family members, this book represents how family capital can be leveraged successfully.) I would also like to acknowledge the important editorial and substantive contributions of Stephen Cranney, PhD, and Joseph Webb and the support of Christopher Robbins, who found my arguments compelling enough to publish the book. And I would like to recognize the Ballard Center for Economic Self-Reliance and the Marriott School of Business for providing much of the research funding needed for the book.

CONTENTS

INTRODUCTION

For over three decades I have taught a college course that focuses on the importance of family-owned businesses. During the course, I have the students look at several case studies of family businesses and ask what gives these businesses a competitive advantage over other firms in their industry. Some of the most common answers are the following:

- » Innovative products
- » Effective manufacturing systems
- » Patents they own
- » Well-trained sales forces
- » Good relationships with suppliers and customers

While these are good answers, almost none of the students initially recognize the critical role that families who own and manage the businesses play in developing a competitive advantage. For some reason, most students tend to believe that families either have little impact on a business or actually undermine business effectiveness due to nepotism and family conflicts. However, recent research has often shown that families—through their skills, commitment, social contacts, and understanding of the marketplace—actually give their businesses a competitive advantage over firms in the same industry with no family connections. Furthermore, if I ask people what assets are most important, most will mention annual income, retirement savings, a job, homes, cars, and other objects—infrequently is family brought up as an important asset. We tend to assume that family is important and that it provides us with support, but we don't view it as an asset we can develop and preserve both for ourselves and other family members. In this book, I'd like to challenge this thinking and suggest the following:

» The family is, or can be, our most valuable asset, not only to help manage a business, but more commonly to help us emotionally, socially, and financially. Family relationships and family support have been shown to be two of the best predictors of our personal happiness and well-being.

» We can do much to strengthen our families and make them valuable assets to be used by ourselves and other family members to better our lives in many different ways. And although we are not competing with other families as in the case of business, the greater our ability to develop, manage, and preserve family resources, the more likely family members will be to thrive and achieve their goals in life as compared to families who don't nurture their family as an asset.

What's Happening to Today's Families?

I have studied and consulted with families and family businesses for the past thirty-five years; I believe families play a significant role in our happiness and the success of society. I have come to one inescapable conclusion: we're in trouble! For the past several decades we have experienced a precipitous decline in what I call *family capital*—the human, social, and financial resources provided by families to family members that help them lead happy, productive, and satisfying lives. This decline in these key family assets has dire consequences for us both now and in the future.

As a family business consultant, I have been particularly interested in the role that families play in the economic, social, and personal well-being of individuals and societies. In the United States, the Waltons, Kochs, Fords, and other such families have controlled many of the leading corporations, creating tremendous wealth for themselves, many of their employees, their shareholders, and society at large. In other countries such as Mexico, virtually all large companies are family-owned and controlled, making family affiliation a significant key to economic success. As I've consulted with highly successful families, I have been impressed by the advantages that family membership gives to its members. Strong families provide an economic and social "safety net" that allows family members to develop and flourish and can provide them with unique opportunities. In this book, I will argue that certain patterns of family structures, cultures, activities, and processes lead to resource-rich families, while other patterns lead to resource-poor families. Moreover, these patterns tend to be intergenerational and are not easy to alter.

The book will show how trends that negatively affect families, if not altered, will have significant repercussions for ourselves and for our communities. I have learned from the successful families I have consulted with how they create and sustain family capital. Their access to family capital leads them to create businesses at higher rates and with a higher degree of success. Moreover, such families produce more resilient children versus children who grow up in families with scarce family capital.

While working with many resource-rich families in my role as the academic director of the Ballard Center for Economic Self-Reliance at my university, I've also been charged to understand and help individuals and families in poverty. I've therefore conducted studies in Mexico, Lithuania, the Palestinian West Bank, and other parts of the world in order to understand how today's resource-poor families struggle to make ends meet. Unfortunately, families with significant resources are the exception rather than the rule in today's world. But I'm also an optimist. Therefore, in this book I provide hope and guidance for those who want to enhance family capital in their own families and provide security for themselves and their loved ones.

My Own Family Background

Because of this book's topic and in the interest of full disclosure, the reader should know my own family background. I am a fifth generation William Dyer. My father's name is William Gibb Dyer and I'm William Gibb Dyer Jr. My son and grandson are sixth and seventh generation William Dyers. I have also been a beneficiary of family capital: my parents provided me with significant emotional, social, and financial support while I was growing up. They helped pay for my undergraduate college education. My father counseled and encouraged me to follow his footsteps in an academic career, and I'm sure his friendship with two faculty members at MIT, Dick Beckhard and Ed Schein, didn't hurt my chances of being admitted to MIT's doctoral program in management. After receiving my PhD I returned to the department my father founded at Brigham Young University in the college where my father served as the dean. Although I believe my career success is due to my own merits, family connections have clearly played an important role. Furthermore, my four siblings, my wife's family, and my extended family have provided me and my wife, Theresa, important social—and at times financial—support over the years (the first car that I shared ownership in, a 1967 Cougar, was brought by Theresa into our marriage).

Theresa and I have been married for over forty years and have seven children: six daughters and one son. Six of the seven are married and I have nineteen grandchildren ranging from age fourteen to just a few months old. In my family line, marriages have generally been quite stable and traditional, but I've been acquainted with a variety of family structures. For example, my great-grandfather John Lye Gibb was a polygamist and had twenty-three children. (After being imprisoned for polygamy in the United States, he moved to Canada with his two wives and children, where there was little enforcement of bigamy laws.) I have several extended family members, close friends, and a daughter who have experienced divorce, so I know the challenges divorce can bring. I've also had good friends in same-sex and cohabiting relationships and other friends and family members who are trying to manage the dynamics of a blended family. My maternal grandmother, Wyroa Hansen, was a single mother most of her life because her husband, Clarence, died at age thirty-six of appendicitis, leaving her with four small children (my mother, Bonnie, was seven months old at the time). My paternal grandmother, Ada Gibb, had a child out of wedlock and raised him as a single mother for seven years until she married. Ada and her husband, George William Dyer, added six more children, including my father. As you read this book, you will learn quite a bit about me and my family since I use examples from my family line to illustrate some family dynamics. Hopefully, my family will not be too embarrassed by the examples I choose—but it's much easier to write from first-hand experience than not.

Concerns

I've had two concerns in writing this book. The first involves clarifying how I feel about the many different types of family structures found in today's world—and my own family, to an extent—ranging from single parent-led families, to blended families, to families led by same-sex couples, to families with heterosexual marriages. I believe all people should value the type of family they find themselves in—we didn't pick the type of family we were born into, and we oftentimes have little control over the kind of family we grow up in or are living in now. I believe all people should value their family members and try, as best they can, to strengthen their family regardless of how it is configured. However, the empirical studies and data presented in the book demonstrate that certain family structures are more amenable to family capital formation than others (with certain exceptions). The more family capital you have, the better. By using social science data and theory, I present facts about the relationship between the various family structures and family capital and the attendant consequences. I also believe that regardless of the kind of family you are a part of, you can do things to create and develop resources for your own family.

The second concern has to do with not wanting to give readers a guilt trip because they don't have the "perfect family." Other families may seem to be doing better than ours as we peruse their pictures of exotic vacations on Facebook or Instagram, but my experience is that all families have significant problems and challenges—we just may not know about them. Many families experience marital conflict, divorce, infidelity, abuse, chronic illness (both physical and mental), or countless other struggles. In my own extended family, substance abuse—mostly in the form of alcoholism—has been a significant problem. Thus, we need to recognize that all families have their flaws. Regardless of the current situation, you can develop and preserve family capital.

The Model of Family Capital and Plan for the Book

The goals of the book are two-fold: to alert you to the sea change regarding families in the United States and worldwide and the serious implications of those changes, and to help you examine your family's situation and see how you might create or strengthen your own family capital.

With these two goals in mind, the book's chapters are designed to focus on how family capital affects countries at the societal level and families at the individual level. In figure 1 is a general model showing the factors that influence family capital along with their outcomes. At the bottom of the model are those societal and individual attitudes toward marriage, child-bearing, divorce, cohabitation, and out-of-wedlock births that have a direct impact on family structure. Family structure not only provides the framework upon which family capital is built but also has the most significant impact on it. However, other factors in the model such as family culture, family activities, family trust, and family-capital transfer activities are also important in developing family resources. Finally, the major outcomes of family capital are business start-up success, family well-being, and individual happiness and well-being. In each box are listed the key factors in the model and the book chapter that discusses them.

Figure 1. Model of Family Capital

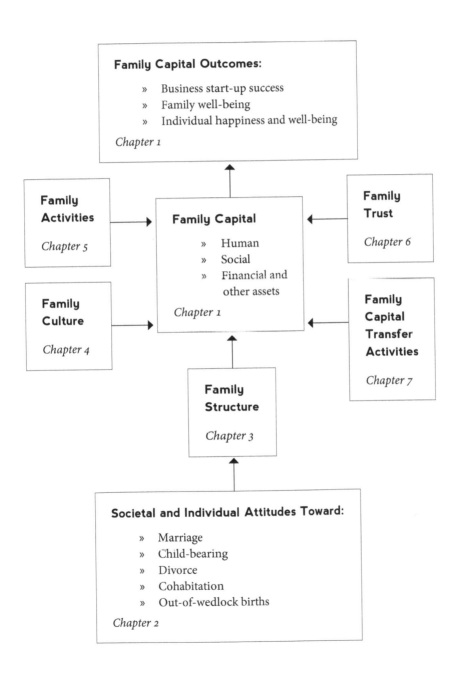

Thus, chapter 1 defines family capital in detail and presents data to demonstrate how a family's human, social, and financial capital are important to launching and growing new enterprises. This chapter focuses on the outcomes of family capital and makes the case for its importance to individuals, families, and societies. Chapter 2 presents data to highlight the fact that key resources needed by families today are in short supply and are declining. The chapter presents statistics regarding marriage and divorce rates, birth rates (and out-of-wedlock birth rates), and cohabitation rates from the United States and selected countries throughout the world and discusses how changes in families over time have affected their ability to garner resources. Chapter 3 presents a series of case studies designed to give the reader a clearer picture of the different kinds of family structures we see today. The picture is generally one of instability, with individuals moving through a variety of family structures during their lifetimes—often to the detriment of themselves, their partners, and their children. Chapter 4 describes the cultural patterns in families that can enhance or undermine the formation of family capital. Families with cultures that foster trust, encourage individual achievement and initiative, and give support and guidance provide fertile soil for growing family capital. Conversely, families with cultures based on distrust, a lack of long-term orientation, and the exploitation of family members are bereft of family assets. Chapter 5 describes how certain family activities—creating a family mission statement, fostering family traditions, and creating opportunities for family members to improve themselves—can be used to enhance family capital. Chapter 6 focuses on how trust is foundational in the development of family resources. The chapter describes not only how trust is frequently lost in families but also how it can be regained to help family members work cooperatively together. It also points out the dark side of familial trust and how it undermines the family. Chapter 7 raises an important issue for all families: how can we transfer family human, social, and financial capital to the next generation? Successful succession planning is the key to preserving family capital—without it, family capital can be lost forever. Chapter 8 covers a subject outside the model, as it describes how churches, schools, nongovernmental organizations (NGOs), and government can substitute for what families provide. Finally, in chapter 9, I present a composite case study based on families I've worked with; it effectively summarizes all the factors in the Family Capital Model and shows what individuals and families can do to create, preserve, and transfer their human, social, and financial capital.

In chapters 1 and 2, I focus primarily on business start-up rates and business success as the major outcomes of family capital because they are tangible, measurable, and important outcomes for individual families and society, and because good data exist regarding business outcomes. However, in subsequent chapters I will discuss how family capital is used in a variety of ways outside of business activity to help family members—for example, providing money for school tuition, loaning a car to help a family member get to work, helping connect family members with potential employers, providing housing for family members temporarily out of work, giving childcare for family members, and furnishing a host of other benefits.

This book presents a plethora of statistics about families in the United States and around the world. Given the variety of data sources, my research team attempted to get the most current and accurate data. Unfortunately, no single repository had all the data we needed. And, in some cases, we found data that were contradictory. In the end, we came up with what we feel are the data that present the most accurate picture of the state of families in the world today. Some of these data are several years old but are based on what we felt were reliable sources.

Because this book aims to give individuals and families specific guidance on how to create, preserve, and transfer family capital, chapters 1, 4, 5, 6, and 7 contain short surveys for you to fill out as a self-check regarding the state of family capital in your own family. I also provide you with important strategies for you and your family to experience the benefits of family capital. While I'm somewhat pessimistic about the role that government and other institutions can play in helping create family capital or providing substitutes for it, I'm very optimistic that individuals and families, if they take certain steps, can be very successful in creating and preserving family capital for themselves and for members of their families.

Family is not an important thing.
It's everything.

Michael J. Fox, actor

CHAPTER 1

WHAT IS FAMILY CAPITAL, AND WHY DO WE NEED IT?

W hether it's solving a Rubik's Cube or the daily crossword puzzle, people like to tackle problems and come up with the right answer. I've been perplexed by a puzzle containing four numbers: 12, 11, 7, and 5. These numbers reflect the average self-employment rates of four different racial groups in the United States in recent years.[1] Asian Americans (12 percent) have had the highest self-employment rate while African Americans (5 percent) have had the lowest, with whites (11 percent) and Hispanics (7 percent) falling in between.[2]

The riddle is: what causes the differences between these four groups? My curiosity was further piqued when I discovered another pair of enigmatic numbers: 24 and 5. The Global Entrepreneurship Monitor (GEM), a worldwide survey of global entrepreneurial activity, noted that 24 percent of the Chinese population are engaged in early start-up activity, but only 5 percent of Russians are similarly engaged.[3] Are the Chinese really five times more entrepreneurial than the Russians, and if so, why?

Additionally, I have been concerned that business start-up rates have been declining in the United States over the past several decades—despite entrepreneurship being touted in the media as the wave of the future and universities putting a much greater emphasis on entrepreneurship in recent years. Start-ups in the US have declined about 20 percent over the past decade; a little over 500,000 start-ups per year existed ten years ago, but only 414,000 in 2015.[4]

Moreover, millennials (those between the ages of twenty and thirty-four) are much less likely to start new businesses than those from previous generations.[5]

As someone who has studied, taught, and researched entrepreneurship and family business for over three decades, I'm supposed to be able to understand and explain why some individuals start businesses that succeed, why others start businesses that fail, and why others don't start businesses at all. When I discuss the possible causes of the differences in self-employment rates between the various racial and ethnic groups with business leaders, colleagues, and students, opinions vary widely. I have been told that Asian Americans, particularly the Chinese, just work harder and have a culture that encourages entrepreneurship; that the long history of discrimination against African Americans has set them back compared to other racial groups; and that Hispanics have an inherent culture of entrepreneurship but have had difficulty gaining financing through banks. Some also say millennials are too soft and thus not well-suited for an entrepreneurial career.

All these explanations are plausible answers to the puzzle. However, they seem rather simplistic and incomplete. In my thirty-plus years of experience working with entrepreneurs and family businesses, I have found what I consider a better answer to this puzzle: *family capital*. Family capital is the human, social, and financial resources available to individuals or groups as a result of family affiliation. When families have these resources available, the process of starting a business becomes easier. Without it, self-employment is difficult, if not impossible. Family capital is more than just a key ingredient in start-up success; it's society's basic building block for wealth-creation and economic prosperity.

In this chapter, after defining some basic terms, I will examine how family capital is created and its advantages. I will then present a case study of one of my clients—Mary Crafts, founder of Culinary Crafts—to describe how she developed family capital within her own family and used it to start and grow her business. I will also describe a study my research team conducted using a large data set to highlight how youths in the United States who have access to family capital are more likely to start successful businesses as compared to youths with less access. This study will focus our attention on the economic implications for societies that lack family capital. At the end of the chapter is a "Family Capital Inventory" so that you can rate your own family along the various dimensions of family capital.

What Is a Family?

Some families have a structure that's typically labeled the "nuclear" or "traditional" family: a married father and mother with children. However, this familial pattern has declined in recent years.[6] Today, we see more blended families as a result of divorce and remarriage, families led by cohabiting partners, families led by a single parent (generally a woman), and families headed by same-sex couples. Moreover, in certain parts of the world, particularly those with a large Muslim population and in tribal Africa, polygamy is a significant family structure. Therefore, I will use the following catch-all definition: a family is comprised of individuals who identify themselves as a family unit, are recognized by others as a family, and share a common biological, genealogical, and/or social history. A possible fourth factor is governmental recognition of these individuals as a family unit, particularly important given that governmental sanction of certain family structures generally provides legal protection for family members. For example, in the case of divorce, the state can require alimony for an ex-partner. However, certain family structures (e.g., same-sex and polygamous) may meet the other three criteria while not being recognized by the state as a family.

Three Types of Family Capital

Fledgling entrepreneurs often have many good ideas but few of the resources needed to turn them into reality. Where can they get the resources to get started? Although entrepreneurs armed with a well-developed business plan can attract money, support, social connections, and other resources from venture capitalists or banks, this is the exception. In most cases, fledgling entrepreneurs are forced to rely on their own resources or on family resources to launch a business.

Primarily three types of family capital (or resources) have been associated with successful start-up activity and self-employment:[7]

> » Skills, knowledge, and labor of family members, or "family human capital"
> » Social connections and reputation shared by family members, or "family social capital"
> » A family's financial and tangible assets, or what I will call "family financial capital"

These three are valuable to family members even if they have no desire to start a business, since family capital can help them in other ways to achieve their individual goals. I will briefly discuss each of the types in turn.

Family Human Capital

Families create human capital by sharing knowledge with family members that can help them in their everyday lives and, in some cases, help them start and run a business.[8] Research has shown that children of self-employed parents are three times more likely to become self-employed than children whose parents are not.[9] Through conversations around the dinner table, summer employment in the family business, or simple observation of their parents, children learn how to create new products, service customers, and make sales. Certain industries such as farming, construction, funeral services, and liquor sales are known for having tried-and-true business tactics that are passed down from generation to generation as family knowledge. The oldest known family business, the Kongō Gumi construction company in Japan, was founded in AD 578 and is being managed by fortieth generation family members.[10] By effectively mentoring younger family members, family elders pass on the secrets of business: how to grow crops, build homes, make tequila, or prepare bodies for burial. One study reported that "business outcomes are 15 to 27 percent better if the owner worked in a family business prior to starting his or her own business."[11] Living in a family business environment would have "a large, positive, and statistically significant effect for all business outcomes."[12]

I've seen these positive effects in my own family. My father, Bill Dyer, worked with his father at the Dyer Grocery store in Portland, Oregon. While delivering groceries, Bill learned a lot about running a small business. He also learned that a career as a grocer was not in his future—the hours were too long and the pay too little. He decided to go to college, earn a PhD, and eventually become a college professor—a career path seen as being viable since his half brother, Jack Gibb, received his PhD in psychology from Stanford University. Bill's academic career began in sociology but changed in the 1960s when Jack introduced him to the new field of organizational behavior. My father began to apply his training in sociology to the field of business and eventually finished his career as dean of the business school at Brigham Young University. As I watched my father over the course of his career, I was attracted to the lifestyle and career opportunities an academic career provided. I was fortunate to do consulting with my father and even took a class from him on change management while I was an MBA student. Moreover, we had countless discussions over the dinner table or while fishing or playing golf about his career, life as a professor, and theoretical and practical issues in business—all of which helped to prepare me for an academic career in the field of management. With this background, both my brother Jeff and I decided to follow our father's footsteps into academia. My son Justin has followed the Dyer family path by becoming an academic as well. What's even more interesting is how closely our research connects us to each other: my father's early work in sociology was on roles and conflict within families, my research and consulting has focused on family businesses, and my son Justin received his PhD in family studies from the University of Illinois. (His dissertation was on how families try to maintain a relationship with an incarcerated father. I have always thought there could be something Freudian about his dissertation topic—maybe Justin had dreams of locking me up in prison after I disciplined him.) The theme of "family" seems to follow the Dyers: I have first-hand experience with family modeling and knowledge sharing.

Family norms of reciprocity (i.e., if I help you, you'll help me) may prompt family members to provide labor needed to carry out a project or help start a business. I've often consulted with siblings, spouses, and other family members who have built a successful business together. A number of years ago, I consulted with General Growth Properties, a billion-dollar real estate construction and investment firm started by Martin and Matthew Bucksbaum. As I worked with Martin and Matthew regarding the issues of succession in their company, I saw that Martin had the skills needed to identify potential locations for new shopping malls. Matthew, on the other hand, was more adept at running the day-to-day affairs of the business. They made an excellent team, a collaboration that would not have been possible without their brotherly connection. By utilizing their family human capital, they eventually built one of the largest real estate development firms in the United States.

Family Social Capital

Family members have unique advantages in developing social capital between family members and their family's stakeholders (e.g., friends, clients, business associates, community leaders) given that they typically cultivate and nurture positive relationships.[13] Family social capital refers to the bonds between family members and those outside the family—relationships that can be used to obtain the resources needed. Family social capital can be even more effective than typical social connections. When outsiders deal with a member of a family that possesses family social capital, they understand that behind that family member stands an entire network of support. Therefore, commitments made by someone representing a family aren't empty promises; obligations are generally shared within the immediate family and may extend to more distant family members as well.

I have found that a unique status is often ascribed to business-owning families, which facilitates important relationships for a family member who wants to start a business. A family's status in the community brings with it certain benefits not available to those outside the family.[14] An example of the impact of family social capital on start-up success can be found in the early story of Microsoft. Founder Bill Gates was able to sell his DOS operating system to IBM because his mother sat on the board of a foundation with the chairman of IBM, John R. Opel, and helped Bill make that connection. So Bill Gates was able to convince IBM to bundle Microsoft's software with its personal computers. Without the help of Bill Gates's mother, Microsoft might not have been able to gain such a dominant position in the software industry.

Family connections also bring advantages to family members by creating a positive reputation for the family in the community, which, in turn, leads to goodwill and trust.[15] An SC Johnson advertisement featuring Fisk Johnson, a fifth-generation Johnson, builds on the family connection: "For years, we've said that SC Johnson is a family company. . . . To us, family is more than a relation. It's our inspiration. Inspiration to care. To try to do what's right. To always be better. Times may have changed since my great-great-grandfather started SC Johnson, but the inspiration behind what we do remains exactly the same."[16] Creating and protecting one's family brand name can help family members gain access to resources they wouldn't obtain otherwise.

Family Financial Capital and Other Assets

Financial capital and other tangible assets for a family business may include office space in the family home, family vehicles, phones, and computers. For example, it's well known that Steve Jobs benefited from his parents' generosity when they allowed him to start Apple in their garage. Scholars David Sirmon and Michael Hitt have noted that a family's "survivability capital"—the pooled financial capital of the family—can help a new business survive and grow. They write, "Survivability capital can help sustain the business during poor economic times. . . . This safety net is less likely to occur in nonfamily firms due to the lack of loyalty, strong ties, or long-term commitments on the part of employees."[17] Family members not only draw upon family financial resources during difficult times but also turn to family members to find start-up money. Such pooling of capital has been instrumental in the proliferation and growth of Chinese family businesses.[18] One study reported that Asian Americans borrow three times more frequently from family and friends than do white Americans.[19] Another study noted that only 7 percent of African Americans borrowed money from spouses, family, or friends to start a new business, but 23 percent of Asian Americans did so.[20] Finally, in their extensive study of start-up rates among racial and ethnic groups in the United States, Robert Fairlie and Alicia Robb, in their book *Race and Entrepreneurial Success*, report that "an important limiting factor" for business start-ups was access to financial capital.[21] Thus, a family's ability to share financial resources with family members is a key factor in business start-up and success.

Distinct Advantages of Family Capital

Family capital tends to be superior to financial, social, and human capital obtained from individuals or institutions outside the family. There are four primary advantages of family capital:

» It is difficult to imitate. In other words, others may not be able to replicate a family's unique resources.

» It can be mobilized quickly.

» It has low transaction costs. Because of high trust within the family, family members probably don't need to put up collateral or involve lawyers to create legal documents when borrowing money or other resources from family members.

» It can be transferred efficiently across generations.

The following hypothetical example illustrates how these advantages play out for members of a family. Roxanne, a recent college graduate with a degree in hospitality management, returns to her hometown intent on starting her very own restaurant. She has a dynamite idea: Roxanne's Restaurant, a cafeteria-style restaurant specializing in Italian cuisine. However, thinking of a good idea is the easy part. To actually get it off the ground, she needs advice, labor, some connections, and some capital. Luckily, she has two ace-in-the-hole connections: her father owns the local hardware store, and she's good friends with the daughter of the president of the largest bank in town. Which connection would more easily help her secure money and support?

Though Roxanne has a connection with the bank president, it won't be so simple borrowing money from his bank. To get a formal meeting with him, Roxanne would likely need to call the president's secretary to set up an appointment. Once in the president's office, she would be greeted warmly; the bank president would assure her that he would do everything in his power to help her. However, there are limits to his control. An informal agreement is very unlikely in this case, as the transaction to obtain seed money would likely take time and require collateral or other security. Significant paperwork may need to be completed, and bank officials may require a formal, possibly lengthy, review before any funds could be released. Moreover, it is unlikely the bank president would be able to quickly and easily transfer his social capital to Roxanne, given that their relationship, though friendly, isn't familial.

Contrast this with Roxanne's connection to her father, the hardware store owner. Roxanne has learned how to start and run a business by watching her father, and likely trusts his judgment. She can set up a meeting with him quickly and obtain readily extended advice and financial help from her father to start her restaurant. If her father is strapped for cash, he can recommend Roxanne to other members of her family who may be willing to invest. Her father might also let her know of an out-of-work cousin with culinary skills who could help her start out at little or no cost. Her father might also introduce her to contacts who could help her launch the new business. Moreover, the family name and reputation might attract customers to the new restaurant.

Though not all families have the kind of relationships that encourage the sharing of human, social, and financial capital within the family—and clearly some nonfamily relations can act in a family-like manner—this example underscores familial advantages.[22]

How Is Family Capital Created?

Certain factors influence the accumulation of, and access to, family capital. Although some factors may seem obvious, it is nevertheless important to describe them explicitly.

Create Stable Family Units

Creating a family is the first requirement of family capital. Marriage (or some other type of union) is central to the formation of a family. Moreover, stable relationships are important to creating family capital, and marriage, although less stable than in years past, typically provides the best opportunity for family stability.

Having Children and a Large Family Network

Family size is an important factor in creating family capital—the more family members available, the more opportunity to create and share resources. However, today's birth rates are at historic lows when compared with birth rates of previous generations. In the past, children were generally seen as assets to help the family economically and to provide support for parents as they aged. But in today's world children are often seen as liabilities: expensive to raise, a lot of work, and limiting the pursuit of other interests. And current birth control measures make it easier to avoid having children. However, despite the expense of raising children, a smaller family typically means less family capital—the larger one's nuclear family and extended family are, the more likely a family member will have access to family capital.

Spending Time Together as a Family

Family members develop bonds of trust and reciprocity as they spend time together. As they work together, whether on household chores or on tasks for a family business, family members learn how to solve problems together, share information and resources, and develop a strong work ethic. Moreover, they develop a norm of reciprocity within the family, which is fundamental to the development of family capital. Additionally, time spent around the dinner table with children is crucial for sharing beliefs, teaching important values, and building stronger relationships.

Opportunities for Family Members to Gain Skills and Education

One final aspect of family functioning that develops family capital is the family's encouragement of formal or informal education that enhances skills and abilities. As the family's combined reservoir of knowledge and skills increases, other members of the family can draw upon that to help them succeed.

I remember one founder of a large clothing manufacturer telling me how his children helped him run his business. He said, "When my sons were in college I told my first son that I needed an accountant in my business; I told my second son that I needed a salesman, and then told my third son that I needed someone with experience in manufacturing. They took my advice to heart and focused their college education in each of these areas. When they finished their degrees, they all had an important role waiting for them in my company. They are now all working for me and are doing well." This father's approach to the career counseling of his sons might appear heavy-handed, but its effectiveness can't be denied. His business now has three trustworthy, hardworking executives with different skill sets that enhance the family's pool of family capital.

Family skills and knowledge can be used in ways beyond just running a business. In my own family, I can turn to family members for legal and medical advice, tips on the housing market, advice about business and insurance, help in doing my taxes, or manual labor to help me move furniture from one room to another. (Now I just need a plumber in the family, but so far no such luck.) This advice and help is typically free and can be accessed quickly.

The Importance of Family Capital: The Culinary Crafts Story

I first met Mary Crafts, founder of Culinary Crafts, in the fall of 2012. Mary was a business acquaintance of my daughter Alison, and Mary confided in Alison that she might need some consulting help with her family business. Her goal was to retire from active management of the business over the course of the next few years, leaving ownership to her two sons, Ryan and Kaleb, who had worked in the business for many years. She also wanted to explore how she might involve her daughter, Meagan, in the business even though Meagan had considerably less experience at Culinary Crafts than her two brothers. When I first met Mary, I was struck by her energy and charisma. I found out later that she had her own cooking show on TV, had catered events for celebrities like Oprah Winfrey, and was widely hailed as the Martha Stewart of the state (minus the felony conviction). Her company, Culinary Crafts, had won the Best of State caterer title for thirteen consecutive years and also won a Caterer of the Year award from the International Caterers Association. I ask all potential clients to tell their story about the start-up and the significant challenges and successes they have experienced. The following is a brief history of Culinary Crafts.

Culinary Crafts quite literally started out as a dream. One night Mary had a vision about a catering company. "I saw it all from beginning to end: how we'd help people through creating wonderful events, how I could build a successful company, and how we were going to be of real service to the community." In 1984, armed with this vision and some money in family savings, Mary and her husband, Ron Crafts, started a small catering business working out of the kitchen in their home. They were conservative in spending as they began the business; their first mixer, a KitchenAid, was a gift from a generous neighbor who felt bad for Ron after learning he had to whip cream by hand. Mary recalls how things were difficult in those early days: "When times were tough, I wondered if we would make it as caterers. I would remember that dream where I saw all those catering vans lined up ready to go out, and I would stay committed to my dream." In the beginning, Mary was trying to build a following and create sales but couldn't afford childcare. As a young boy, Ryan would tag along and pull the Radio Flyer wagon full of breads, cookies, and other baked goods while Mary sold door-to-door. Soon he was tasked with tending the company's herb and vegetable gardens. Ryan's little brother Kaleb also started at an early age. One evening, Mary had no choice but to bring an eleven-year-old Kaleb to an event at the last minute and found the perfect job to keep him occupied: standing at the end of the buffet table and pointing guests in the direction of the dessert table. Mary gave him two simple instructions: say, "The dessert table is this way" and point in the correct direction. He performed beautifully—so much so that Mary didn't go back right away to check on him. After all the guests had gone through the buffet line, she realized that Kaleb must be standing there with nothing to do. She quickly ran to the table, but Kaleb wasn't there. She found him over at the dessert table, politely describing to the guests each dessert, recommending the ones that were his favorites, and proudly proclaiming that they were all made from scratch!

Over time, Ryan moved up the Culinary Crafts chain, working as dishwasher, one of the event setup crew, grill master, event manager, fleet manager, accounts payable and payroll clerk, and more. He currently works as president and chief operating officer and is responsible for company events and menus—Culinary Crafts clients come back because Ryan knows how to put on a great event. Kaleb gravitated to the sales side of the business and is currently the president of sales and marketing. He is particularly adept at corporate sales and secured a strong business relationship with the prestigious, popular Sundance Film Festival. Ryan and Kaleb purchased 49 percent of the company from Mary in 2013 and the remaining 51 percent in 2018.

Mary is proud to share the spotlight with her sons. She explains, "We've reached a point where Culinary Crafts is no longer just the 'Mary Show,' it's the result of an entire catering team doing an incredible job day in and day out." Mary continues, "Ryan and Kaleb grew up in the business. They know it inside and out and they are very good at what they do!" Daughter Meagan has been tasked with creating unique event decor, working on internal HR campaigns, and supervising on-site cooking. She is now stepping into business administration duties; as the marketing coordinator, she implements all marketing and social media campaigns. Her husband, Clayton Price, served for a number of years as an expert event manager. He now serves as the director of event operations, training all the service staff to maintain company quality standards. Jen Crafts, Ryan's wife, is responsible for website updates and photo archives. Mary has cultivated a veritable army of skilled family members to help her both launch and grow the business.

One hiccup in the process of creating and growing Culinary Crafts was Mary's divorce from Ron in 2010. Ron left the business in 2008 as a result of various personal and family issues. As business partners both Ron and Mary owned 50 percent of the business. As part of the divorce agreement, Mary decided that she would buy out Ron and become the sole owner, which happened in 2010. While this was quite painful for Mary both financially and emotionally, the company has continued to grow after Mary's divorce from Ron. The business has started its fourth decade as a premier caterer and Mary and her family recently built and moved into a new 16,500-square-foot catering facility.

The story of Culinary Crafts helps us better understand how family capital is created and used to foster the successful launch of a business. Family savings and the use of the family kitchen were key resources that enabled the business to get started. Mary and Ron also had baking skills that led to the firm's initial success, and later on, the business leaned heavily on the labor of Mary's children. Rather than being forced to spend their limited capital on hiring and training employees, Mary and Ron were able to raise children that had the necessary skills to help Culinary Crafts grow. Furthermore, Mary's reputation and social capital in the community was enhanced by her TV appearances and culinary acumen, which created a positive image for Mary, her family, and her business. The Craft's path to success is not easy to copy, as competitors can't easily mimic thirty years of parenting, teaching, and family togetherness.

How Family Capital Affects Start-up Success in the United States: The NLSY97 Study

A few studies have looked at relationships between family members and start-up *activity*, but little in-depth research has been done exploring the relationship between family capital and start-up *success*.[23] To focus on this issue, my colleagues and I developed two hypotheses:

> » Youths with access to family capital will start more businesses than those youths without access to family capital.
> » The businesses of those youths who have a comparative advantage in family capital will survive longer and make more money than the businesses founded by youths with less family capital.

To test these hypotheses, we analyzed data from the National Longitudinal Survey of Youth (NLSY97) conducted by the US Census. This unique data set gave us the ability to assess the family capital of over 8,000 randomly selected twelve- to sixteen-year-olds *before* they launched a business, observe if and when they started new enterprises, and measure the success of their businesses over time.[24] During the fourteen-year duration of the study (1997 to 2010), 24 percent of the youths started a business while 76 percent did not.

To conduct our study, we created a baseline of the youths' family capital when they were initially surveyed. We measured family human capital based on the parents' education levels and whether or not the parents had been self-employed, reasoning that these measures reflected the skills and background that could be accessed by the youths. Family financial capital was measured by household annual net income and the total dollar amount of loans to the youth from the family, which measured the amount of money youths borrowed or might potentially borrow from family members. To measure family social capital, we used two questions. First, the youths were asked to rate their parents' support of them, which essentially indicates how close the youths were to their parents and how much they could rely on them for help. The second asked youths to indicate the number of loans given them by family members, which shows whether the family is connected enough to repeatedly loan each other money. You'll notice that this is a similar question to the one posed for family financial capital; we reasoned that the total amount of the loans would more likely measure the family's financial resources while number of loans given to the youth would indicate the level of trust and social capital within the family. The variables in the NLSY97 aren't perfect, but reasonably represent the three types of family capital. These variables largely focus on the parents' impact on the youth—the parents' education and business experience, their wealth, and their relationship with the youth.[25]

To obtain a more comprehensive view of entrepreneurial success for each youth in the study, we performed what is called "latent profile analysis" (LPA), which helped us identify "clusters" of entrepreneurs based on various criteria of success.[26] Rather than use a simple unidimensional measure of success (for instance, "annual income"), which many entrepreneurship studies employ, our clustering allowed us to identify seven unique groups of youths based on the following three criteria: the number of businesses started by the youth by the year 2010, the number of weeks the youth was self-employed from 2000 to 2010, and self-employment income from wages and business profit from 2000 to 2010. Thus, by our measures of success, youths who launched fewer businesses that fared poorly and survived for only short periods were less successful than those who started more enterprises that experienced significant growth over longer periods. The characteristics of the various clusters and their entrepreneurial outcomes are found in table 1.1 (on the following page) and here, in a more graphical representation, in figure 1.1.[27]

Figure 1.1 The Relationship Between Family Capital and Business Success

Table 1.1 Comparative Advantage of Family Capital of NLSY Youth from 1997 to 2010

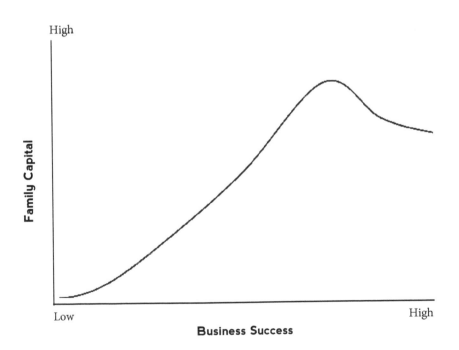

Descriptions of the Clusters

Cluster Name	% of Sample	Total Self-Employment Income Mean	Number of Start-ups	Weeks Self-Employed	Family Capital Competitive Advantage Over Other Clusters*
1. Non-Entrepreneur	76%	0	0	0	None
2. Struggling Entrepreneur	6.5%	$27,460	1.26	46.6	Low
3. Seasonal Entrepreneur	6.1%	$14,478	1	12.2	High
4. Short-Term Entrepreneur	4.9%	$97,155	1.49	109.6	High
5. Successful Entrepreneur	3.5%	$344,753	1.77	195.3	Very High
6. Star Entrepreneur	1.9%	$1,917,505	1.83	344.5	Medium
7. Superstar Entrepreneur	1.1%	$1,512,184	1.36	70.2	Medium

*Number of competitive advantages in family capital over another cluster: Low—1, Medium—2-3, High—4-6, Very High—7

Cluster 1 youths are those who were *non-entrepreneurs*—those who didn't start a business *(#1)*. This cluster represents 76 percent of the entire sample.

Cluster 2 (6.5 percent of the total sample, 27 percent of the entrepreneurs) I labeled as *struggling entrepreneurs (#2)*. These individuals were self-employed for an average of only forty-six weeks and started an average of 1.26 businesses, with total mean income at $27,460. In short, these entrepreneurs were not successful.

Cluster 3 (6.1 percent of the sample, 25 percent of the entrepreneurs) youths fit the profile of a *seasonal entrepreneur (#3)*. They started exactly one business, were self-employed for about three months (a typical summer vacation period), and made a reasonable income ($14,478) for the time they were self-employed.

Cluster 4 (4.9 percent of the sample, 20 percent of the entrepreneurs) youths were called *short-term entrepreneurs (#4)* since they were self-employed for just over two years. They started an average of one and a half businesses and made an average of $886 per week, or about $46,000 per year (or $97,155 total self-employment income).

Cluster 5 (3.5 percent of the sample, 15 percent of the entrepreneurs) was labeled *successful entrepreneurs (#5)*. They started 1.77 businesses on average and were self-employed for almost four years (195 weeks). Their average weekly income was $1,765 making an average annual income of $91,780 for a total income of $344,753 while they were self-employed.. Thus they made almost twice as much annually as the short-term entrepreneurs.

Cluster 6 (1.9 percent of the sample, 8 percent of the entrepreneurs) was comprised of what we called *star entrepreneurs (#6)*. They started 1.83 businesses on average and were self-employed for over six and a half years—they had significant staying power. Average weekly income was $5,566 making their average annual income $289,432 ($1,917,505 average total). Such an income suggests that they were highly competent in the role of a self-employed entrepreneur.

Cluster 7 (1.1 percent of the sample, 5 percent of the entrepreneurs) youths were designated *superstar entrepreneurs (#7)*. They started fewer businesses (1.36) than clusters 4, 5, and 6 and were self-employed for a significantly shorter time period than clusters 4–6 (only 70.2 weeks). However, they generated significant wealth in this short time span—$21,525 per week or about $1.5 million in income for being self-employed for less than a year and a half. Thus they fit the profile of entrepreneurs who found "hyper-growth" businesses.

After identifying the youths in each of the seven clusters and identifying their access to family capital, we found the following:[28,29]

»   Youths with no statistically significant comparative advantage in family capital don't start businesses. The data clearly show that family capital does matter when one contemplates starting a business.

»   Youths who launch a business but rated "low" in family capital are likely to fail (i.e., cluster #2).

»   Family capital gives youths a comparative advantage in the success of their businesses. Youths with a medium to high comparative advantage in family capital fared better.

However, table 1.1 also shows that highly successfully youth entrepreneurs—#6, star entrepreneurs, and #7, superstar entrepreneurs—had fewer advantages in family capital when compared with clusters 3, 4, and 5. Clusters 6 and 7 represent a small subset of the youths (only 3 percent of the entire sample and 13 percent of the entrepreneurs), and I suspect these highly successful entrepreneurs, while having some advantages in family capital, may also have found resources outside their families to help their businesses grow rapidly. For example, in 2016 my son-in-law Denver Lough left his plastic-surgery residency at Johns Hopkins Hospital to start his biotech company, PolarityTE, and needed millions of dollars to launch the business. Because our family and Denver's family didn't have that kind of money, he turned to venture capital funding. However, I did introduce Denver to my brother Jeff, a strategy professor with contacts in the venture capital industry, who helped connect Denver with venture capitalists and also helped prepare him to make presentations to the venture capitalists to get funding. Denver also turned to his wife—Mary, my daughter—to help him launch the business since she has a background in the medical field. My daughter Christine and her husband, Peter, have also worked for the firm in a legal/human resource role and a facilities management role, respectively. Thus, PolarityTE was started with both family capital and external funding and support. In the case of rapidly growing businesses that need resources over and above what the family has to offer, we're likely to see a mix of family and external resources that determine business success. But again, these types of firms represent a small minority of the start-ups (13 percent). The vast majority of successful start-ups (60 percent) had significant family resources to draw upon.

Our study of entrepreneurship among America's youth points out the importance of family capital to youths who want to start a business. Those youths who had well-educated, supportive parents with a knowledge of business and who also had family members willing to lend them money appeared to be best prepared to launch a business. After they started their businesses, those youths who had access to family capital performed better over time. Thus, our study, which is highly representative of the youth of America, emphasizes the importance of family capital for business start-up and success.

More Common Uses of Family Capital

Family capital also plays an important role in one's family, unrelated to starting a business. For example, in one family, which we'll call the Thomas family, John Thomas felt he wasn't progressing in his career at the high-tech company where he worked. His father, while discussing the situation with his son, noted that his good friend had just started a high-tech company and needed someone with John's skills. John's father helped set up the interview with his friend and John was eventually offered the job. John needed to relocate several hundred miles for this new position, so family members helped John and his wife Erica pack up and move (John's parents also helped him with moving expenses) and John's brother offered to let John and Erica stay with his family while they looked for a new home. After several months of living with John's brother and saving up money for a down payment, John and Erica found an ideal place to live and shortly thereafter had a baby girl, Jean. John's mother now watches Jean several days each week so that Erica can continue working and also help provide for the family. In John's case, his family's human, social, and financial capital didn't help him start a business, but contributed to a much better financial position and career path. And as John and his family build their family capital over time, they will similarly be able to help other family members.

The Family Capital Inventory

As I began writing this book I wondered how much family capital the Dyer family has. Do we have "sufficient" human, social, and financial capital to help family members in time of need or help them start a business? Does my family have ways to talk about family capital and share it if needed? So I created a survey to help assess the ability of a family to create and preserve family capital. This survey is included at the end of this chapter.

Chapter Takeaways

» Family capital is composed of the human, social, and financial capital in a family.

» Family capital is generated when family units are created, children are born, and there are stable family relationships.

» Family capital is important for business startup success and family members' well-being.

Survey 1: Family Capital Inventory

1. How many people do you know personally whom you consider to be family members (including extended family)?

0–10	11–30	31–60	61–100	101+
1	2	3	4	5

2. How many hours do you spend each week interacting with family members?

0	1–10	11–20	21–50	51+
1	2	3	4	5

3. In general, to what extent do you consider your family members to be well-educated (include both formal and informal education)?

Not well educated			*Highly educated*	
1	2	3	4	5

4. To what extent do your parents or other family members have experience in operating a business or are in a career similar to yours?

Very little extent			*To a great extent*	
1	2	3	4	5

5. To what extent does your family have a positive reputation?

Very little extent			*To a great extent*	
1	2	3	4	5

6. To what extent does your family help family members by sharing knowledge or social contacts, or providing labor (e.g., helping a family member to move)?

Very little extent			*To a great extent*	
1	2	3	4	5

7. To what extent do you feel emotional support from members of your family?

Very little extent   *To a great extent*

1   2   3   4   5

8. To what extent does your family have resources (i.e., money, a home, computers, vehicles, tools, work space, equipment, etc.) that could be used to start a business or support a family member in need?

Very little extent   *To a great extent*

1   2   3   4   5

9. If you needed to buy something that was very important, to what extent would a family member (or family members) be willing to loan you the money?

Very little extent   *To a great extent*

1   2   3   4   5

10. Approximately how much, in total, could you potentially borrow from family members for something very important to you?

$0   *Up to $1K*   *$1K–$15K*   *$15K–$50K*   *$50K+*

1   2   3   4   5

Scoring: Add your scores from each of the ten questions. The following totals approximate where your family is in terms of family capital.

» 41–50 High degree of family capital
» 31–40 Moderately high degree of family capital
» 20–30 Moderate degree of family capital
» <20 Relatively low degree of family capital

Notes

1. Self-employment rates among the various racial groups have fluctuated slightly in recent years, with Hispanics making some gains. However, Asian Americans still create the most successful new businesses.

2. Robert W. Fairlie and Alicia M. Robb, *Race and Entrepreneurial Success* (Cambridge: MIT Press, 2008).

3. D. Kelley, S. Singer, and M. Harrington, *Global Entrepreneurship Monitor:* 2015–16.

4. R. J. Samuelson, *Washington Post*, October 8, 2017.

5. J. D. Harrison, "The Decline in American Entrepreneurship—in Five Charts," (February 12, 2015), https://www.washingtonpost.com.

6. Mary Eberstadt, *How the West Really Lost God*, (West Conshohocken, PA: Templeton Press, 2013).

7. S. M. Danes et al. "Family Capital of Family Firms: Bridging Human, Social, and Financial capital," *Family Business Review* 22 no. 3 (2009): 199–215.

8. To examine how different races approach child-rearing to develop human capital in a family see A. Lareau, *Unequal Childhoods: Race, Class, and Family Life* (Berkeley, CA: University of California Press, 2011).

9. Fairlie and Robb, *Race and Entrepreneurial Success.*

10. Company website is www.kongogumi.co.jp.

11. Fairlie and Robb, *Race and Entrepreneurial Success*, 179.

12. Fairlie and Robb, *Race and Entrepreneurial Success,* 92.

13. Thomas M. Zellweger et al., "Building a Family Firm Image: How Family Firms Capitalize on Their Family Ties," *Journal of Family Business Strategy* 3 (2012): 239–250.

14. Marc-David L. Seidel, Jeffrey T. Polzer, and Katherine J. Stewart, "Friends in High Places: The Effects of Social Networks on Discrimination in Salary Negotiations," *Administrative Science Quarterly* 45 no. 1 (2000): 1–24.

15. W. Gibb Dyer Jr., "Examining the 'Family Effect' on Firm Performance," *Family Business Review* 19 no. 4 (2006): 253–273.

16. *Parade Magazine*, May 2, 2010.

17. David G. Sirmon and Michael A. Hitt, "Managing Resources: Linking Unique Resources, Management, and Wealth Creation in Family Firms," *Entrepreneurship: Theory and Practice* 27 no. 4 (2003): 339–358.

18. Francis Fukuyama, *Trust: The Social Virtues and the Creation of Prosperity* (New York: Free Press, 1995).

19. Timothy Bates, *Race, Self-Employment, and Upward Mobility: An Elusive American Dream* (Washington, DC: Woodrow Wilson Center Press, 1997).

20. United States Census, 1987.

21. Fairlie and Robb, *Race and Entrepreneurial Success*, 107.

22. W. Gibb Dyer, Elizabeth Nenque, and E. Jeffrey Hill, "Toward a Theory of Family Capital and Entrepreneurship: Antecedents and Outcomes," *Journal of Small Business Management* 52 no. 2 (2014): 266–285.

23. Manfred F. R. Kets de Vries, "The Dark Side of Entrepreneurship," *Harvard Business Review* 63 no. 6 (1985): 160–167.

24. Prior studies have typically relied on data from the Survey of Businesses Owners (SBO), the Characteristics of Business Owners (CBO), the Survey of Minority-Owned Business Enterprises (SMOBE) and the Current Population Survey (CPS). These studies typically

looked at entrepreneurs after they started their businesses thus biasing the sample toward those who have already chosen an entrepreneurial career.

25. J. K. Vermunt and J. Magidson, "Latent Class Cluster Analysis," in *Applied Latent Class Analysis*, eds. J. A. Hagenaars and A. L. McCutcheon (Cambridge, UK: Cambridge University Press, 2002): 89–106.

26. As control variables we included the youths' age, marital status, gender, education, and race as well as the industries in which the youths started their businesses and whether or not their parents were divorced.

27. Once the clusters were identified, multinomial logistic regression was used to examine the predictors of the various classes and thus enabled us to include proper controls into the models. To determine the number of unique clusters, various fit statistics were examined to see what number of clusters best fit the data. The most common fit statistics are the Bayesian information criterion (BIC), the sample-size adjusted BIC (SABIC), and Akaike's information criterion (AIC). The lower these numbers, the better the model fits the data. These analyses examine at what point adding additional clusters decreases the model fit. In addition to examining these fit criteria, we also examined the clusters to determine if they were conceptually distinct from each other. LPA fit statistics may indicate a model fits better with an additional cluster; however, the additional cluster may simply represent the tail end of another cluster and not actually be categorically distinct. We examined the fit of models specifying from one to nine clusters. In examining fit statistics, we found that for each fit statistic (BIC, SABIC, and AIC) at no point did the model worsen with the addition of clusters (not uncommon when dealing with large amounts of data). However, after the six-cluster model, model fit improved only minimally (< 2 percent) with each additional cluster, though it was found that adding the seventh cluster added a conceptually distinct group.

After creating the seven clusters, additional cluster sizes were less than 1 percent of the sample. In addition, the eighth and ninth clusters are likely the tail end of the seventh cluster. These two clusters were apparently "broken off" of the seventh cluster (i.e., when adding the eighth and ninth clusters, the size of all the other clusters remained unchanged except for the seventh cluster, which was reduced by the size of these two clusters). Given that the eighth and ninth clusters were less than 1 percent of the sample and represented the extreme tail-end of the highly successful entrepreneurs, we determined not to retain them as unique clusters but kept them subsumed within the seventh cluster. The seven-cluster solution was therefore designated as our final model.

The seven-cluster solution fit the data very well. For LPA, determining the degree of uncertainty in classifying individuals is important. Entropy is a common measure of this, ranging from 0–1, with values closer to 1 representing fewer errors in classification. Although .8 is often considered an acceptable value, the seven-cluster model had an entropy score of .98 representing a very small amount of uncertainty in classification. In other words, the seven-cluster model was able to classify individuals in the sample with a high degree of accuracy.

28. We used a multinomial logistical regression technique and compared each of the seven clusters to one another to see if there was a statistically significant difference between the clusters.

29. To test our hypotheses we conducted a multinomial logistic regression where cluster membership was the outcome (i.e., an unordered categorical variable representing which cluster each participant belonged to) and each of the predictors were independent variables. Thus, we could examine how each predictor related to cluster membership (i.e., cluster membership was the dependent variable) while controlling for all of the other predictors. To compare each cluster with each other cluster, the base category was simply switched. Thus, we needed to run the multinomial regression six times, each specifying a different base category.

Our initial hypotheses were generated without the benefit of knowing the detailed descriptions of the seven clusters—it is difficult to predict a priori how many clusters will be generated and their distinguishing characteristics. However, our hypotheses were tested via paired-comparison analysis with a more nuanced understanding of the data given that we compared each cluster with all of the other clusters related to the hypotheses we were testing.

Those economies that will advance most rapidly will tend to have strong family structures.

Gary Becker, Nobel Prize-winning economist

CHAPTER 2

HOW WE ARE LOSING FAMILY CAPITAL

With the understanding that family capital contributes to business success and fuels national economic growth, let's examine those societal trends influencing and oftentimes undermining the development of family capital today: marriage rates, fertility rates, divorce rates, cohabitation rates, and out-of-wedlock birth rates. In this chapter I will describe the impact of these five factors on family capital and then present data from the four major racial groups in the United States—whites, African Americans, Hispanics, and Asian Americans—as to how they fare along these five factors. These data will help answer the self-employment puzzle described in chapter 1. Later on, I will examine how certain countries worldwide are faring with these trends.

Marriage Rates

Marriage provides several direct sources of family capital, the most obvious being human capital. When starting a business, spouses frequently provide labor and at times important expertise (often unpaid) to help a new business grow.[1] Social connections or financial resources that a spouse brings to a marriage can also prove crucial in starting a new enterprise or solving a variety of problems. Data from several sources indicate firms founded by married entrepreneurs are likely to have more staying power than those founded by entrepreneurs who are not married.[2] This is likely because entrepreneurs are more willing to take risks and can remain in business longer if their spouses also have incomes and can provide health insurance. The employed spouse provides not only a financial safety net but also a "psychological safety net" of encouragement and support during difficult times. Psychological support is important even if one is not starting a business. An early study of Asian and Latino immigrants to the United States found that "being married and living with the spouse increases the odds of self-employment for each ethnic group."[3] For men and women, being married increases the chance of self-employment by 20 percent.[4] I sometimes tell my students, "If you really want to be a successful entrepreneur, get married first!"

Entrepreneurs definitely have challenges managing work-family relationships, but many of my consulting clients have been successful both in marriage and business. A study I conducted several years ago noted that over 80 percent of entrepreneurs surveyed were "quite satisfied" or "very satisfied" with their marriages.[5] A successful entrepreneur I know well, Steve Gibson, sold his oxygen business and then partnered with his wife Bette in a new social venture. They now work with poor young people in the Philippines and Mexico, training them to start new enterprises since traditional employment isn't generally available. Steve has always said that Bette's support was important to him in launching a successful entrepreneurial career, and they are now partners in their social venture.

Recent demographic trends in the United States, however, point to a decline in marriage rates and thus the advantages that can accompany marriage. In the United States the average age at first marriage in 1970 was 22.5 years old for men and 20.5 for women; in 2017 it was 29.5 (men) and 27.4 (women).[6] In terms of percentages, in 1960 about 70 percent of Americans over the age of fifteen were married; by 1990, the numbers had fallen to 61 percent and by 2017 the percentage was 54 percent.[7] Today fewer Americans access family capital through marriage than ever before. A few years ago I heard one woman in her forties complain: "I just saw the statistics. It's more likely that I'll be killed by a terrorist than find a man to marry!" Her overdramatization notwithstanding, clearly, in the United States young people are delaying marriage until their mid to late twenties. One study reported that one in seven adult Americans has decided to forgo marriage completely.[8]

Fertility Rates

Compared with today, birth rates in previous generations were relatively high, as children were seen as economic assets to help on the farm or in the father's line of work. Not all children lived to maturity, and having many children provided a hedge against the potential loss of a child due to illness, injury, or death. In the case of my own family, my grandmother Ada Dyer had seven children who all lived to maturity, and her mother Sarah Gibb had thirteen children, four of which died in infancy. But due to the recent trend of smaller families, one study noted that this decline in family size hinders entrepreneurial activity: "Individuals from smaller-sized families may perceive that they have inadequate potential resources available from kin members, and thus decide against starting their own firm."[9]

Another study reported that 25 percent of the firms in their sample employed family members at the time of start-up.[10] Moreover, "the larger . . . [the] family units, the larger the pool of people from whom small entrepreneurs might borrow."[11] One example of this is the Amish community, where couples with ten children are not uncommon. Thus, an Amish person could have 90 first cousins (180 if you count the spouse's first cousins), "each of whom is available as a potential lender."[12] Finally, another study reported that although family members may not loan money they could help make connections with people and institutions that have money to lend.[13]

My own family history provides a rather extreme example: my great-grandfather, John Lye Gibb, was born in England in 1848 and married Sarah Silcox, with whom he had thirteen children. They emigrated to the United States where, led by religious beliefs, Sarah and John asked Hannah Simmons to become John's second wife in a polygamous marriage. This new wife added ten more children to the Gibb family, for a total of twenty-three. After being imprisoned for six months for polygamy, John Lye Gibb moved his family to southern Alberta, Canada, where bigamy laws were not enforced. There he became a prominent businessman, as his ten sons who lived to maturity helped him run the "John Lye Gibb and Sons" shoe and harness company. Thus polygamy, deemed barbaric by some, provided important human capital for my great-grandfather.

Association with entrepreneurial family members and working in the family business are two of the best predictors of future start-up activity and subsequent success; family size increases the opportunity for such experiences. Besides the increased likelihood of starting a business, a child (or other relative) working in the family business prior to starting her own will find that experience to have a positive impact on the business she starts.[14]

But finding family members to work with may prove more difficult in the future. Total fertility rates have plummeted in the United States in recent years, from 3.65 in 1960 to 2.48 in 1970 to 1.84 in 1980; 2017 saw the lowest birth rate in US history—1.77 children per woman, solidly below replacement rate.[15]

Divorce Rates

I am aware of cases in which a husband and wife working together in a business get a divorce but are able to still work amicably together—and apparently still share the various forms of family capital. However, all too often divorce significantly damages family capital. Research has stressed the importance of transferring social capital to your children in order to help them succeed.[16] Since divorce often disrupts ties between parents and children, that becomes more difficult. Divorce also makes it more difficult for families to work together. Fairlie and Robb report that "having only one parent at home limits potential exposure to family business, particularly if the absent parent is the father."[17] Divorce can also undermine trust between parents and children, since children generally grow up believing their parents will always be together. Violated expectations lead to distrust. Paul Amato, a highly regarded sociology professor at Penn State University, in reviewing the literature on divorce, notes that "children in divorced families tend to have weaker emotional bonds with mothers and fathers than do their peers in two-parent families."[18] If emotional distance or distrust become part of the family dynamics, likely fewer family members would work in a business together, and if they did, conflicts would probably spill over into the business. Poorer firm performance and fewer family firms transferring to the next generation would result, since the founders' children would have had little or no association with the business.

Divorce also can have a negative impact on the family human capital inasmuch as it affects a family member's ability to function effectively and be a significant contributor to the family. Professor Amato explains some of the risk factors associated with divorce: "Children with divorced parents continued to have lower average levels of cognitive, social, and emotional well-being, even in a decade in which divorce had become more common and widely accepted."[19] Moreover, divorce has also been correlated with increased drug use by the children of divorced parents.[20] Whereas substance abuse has many causes other than family disruption, it has a devastating impact on family capital, draining families financially, physically, emotionally, and even spiritually. In 2017, over seventy thousand people died in the United States from a drug overdose, which is about fifteen thousand more than the number of American servicemen and women who died during the entire Vietnam War.[21] Thus, drug addiction touches virtually everyone in American today and most homes throughout the world. To avoid this scourge, families need to provide a stable and nurturing environment for children to flourish, and also provide needed support when family members struggle. Stable families create stronger people who can turn to their families for support rather than turn to drugs or alcohol to cope with their problems.

Furthermore, several studies indicate that the cognitive, emotional, and behavioral problems of children of divorced parents often don't improve if the parents remarry and the child becomes a member of a blended family.[22] And family financial capital is also undermined through a divorce since family assets are divided between spouses and cannot be pooled to start a business or support family members. Divorce often triggers economic hardship in the family.

One day, early in my career, I received a phone call from an entrepreneur who heard that I was a family business consultant. He wanted to have lunch with me to ask a few questions about his family business. I'm always up for a free meal, so we met at a local hotel the next week for what I thought would be a short lunch. After a few minutes seated at the table, the man said, "I guess you're wondering why I asked you to lunch. Well, I've had a problem with my family business: I fired my son a couple of weeks ago because I felt he was doing something unethical in the business. My wife is so mad that she's kicked me out of the house and I'm sleeping on a couch at my office. Can you help me?" As you might suspect, his problem is not a typical one that I encounter. I encouraged the man to get some professional marriage counseling, but I also felt I could help him improve how he worked with family members in his business. After a few weeks I helped him rehire his son and he was back sleeping in his own bed. However, the family relationships remained very volatile as I consulted with this entrepreneur and his family over the next several years. Eventually, as the marriage broke down, the couple got a divorce. When dividing up the assets of the business, they realized the business had to be sold. It was, the family fractured, and my lunch companion died alone several years later, in a place far from home and the location of the former family business. The divorce undermined much of the family capital that the family had built up over the years.

The United States is experiencing an era of historically high divorce rates. The number of divorces per 1,000 married women in 1960 was 9.2. The divorce rate rose sharply to 14.9 per 1,000 in 1970 and peaked at 22.6 in 1980; it showed a slight decline in 1990 to 20.9 and has leveled out at 16.4 in 2009 (which translates into about 45 percent of first marriages ending in divorce).[23] The stabilization of the divorce rate in the United States is likely due to the following:

» Tougher economic conditions that make staying together a better financial option.
» Cohabitation among those likely to be poorer marriage partners, so that divorce becomes unnecessary when the couple splits.

Cohabitation Rates

Cohabitation, or living together in an emotionally and/or sexually intimate relationship, is most often viewed as a stepping-stone toward marriage rather than as an alternative to it. However, research indicates that cohabitation fails to provide couples with many marriage benefits, including family capital. When compared in the aggregate to married couples, cohabiters have poorer physical and mental health,[24] less happiness,[25] a lower-quality relationship with their partners,[26] decreased productivity at work,[27] and shorter longevity.[28] Research particularly pertinent to family capital indicates that couples in a cohabiting relationship have poorer relationships with their parents[29] and are not as connected to the larger community (such as in-laws and churches) as are married individuals.[30] Cohabiters are also less likely to pool their resources and work together to meet financial or career goals.[31] In essence, they act more as individuals than as a couple. Another study also found that children of cohabiting parents had more behavioral and emotional problems and lower school attainment than did children of married parents.[32] Also, if the cohabiting male is not the biological father to the children, there is a much greater likelihood of sexual or physical abuse.[33] If a child's emotional health is compromised, he or she may be less able to contribute to family capital in the future.

Cohabitation rates have dramatically increased during the last several decades. The number of cohabiting couples in the United States increased thirty-five-fold between 1960 and 2010.[34] Additionally, serial cohabitation (cohabitating with several different people over time) increased by over 40 percent over the past twenty years.[35] Recent US data show that 14.7 percent of females and 13.3 percent of males cohabited between 2011 and 2015, a 63 percent increase for the women and a 33 percent increase for the men since 2002.[36]

Cohabitation can sound like a good idea to individuals exploring a long-term relationship, but it can actually undermine relationship stability. Cohabiters marry about 50 percent of the time, but when they do marry, most studies indicate they are much more likely to divorce than those who did not live together before they were married.[37] As compared to married couples, cohabiters break up more frequently (married couples stay together 2.5 times longer than cohabiting couples), and 80 percent of the children of cohabiting couples will spend some of their lifetime living in a single parent home.[38] Moreover, about half of the children who have experienced divorce in their own families cohabit before they marry (between 54 percent and 62 percent) while only 29 percent of children with parents who stayed married decided to cohabit before marriage.[39] That is probably because children of divorce may hesitate to marry given their negative experience and thus see cohabitation as a reasonable alternative.

Out-of-Wedlock Births

The Fragile Families Study based at Princeton University summarizes the risk factors associated with children born to unwed parents: they are less healthy on average at birth, often grow up in poverty, experience more anxiety and depression, have more behavioral problems, and do poorly in school, as compared to their peers with two married parents.[40] Although exceptions clearly exist—my maternal grandmother raised four healthy children after her husband died of appendicitis in his early thirties, for example—in general, children raised with only one parent tend to have a more disrupted home life. Furthermore, because their family capital is typically limited to the resources of one parent, they have fewer familial resources to draw upon (as compared to two-parent families). My mother told me many stories about the challenges growing up in the Great Depression with the family's only income coming from her mother, a first-grade school teacher. Her family never owned a home growing up—they rented a small apartment attached to the landlord's home—and my grandmother often had to rely on credit from the local grocer to keep her family fed. As a ten-year-old child, my mother was sent by her mother to the local grocery store to pick up some groceries, only to be denied the food because her mother was delinquent on her account. While my grandmother did the best she could, it was difficult to provide for four young children during the Great Depression.

The percentage of out-of-wedlock births in the United States has skyrocketed in the last several decades, from 5 percent of all births in the 1960s to 41 percent in 2009.[41] (Non-marital births, while remaining at historically high levels, have declined slightly in recent years.[42]) Much of the increase in out-of-wedlock births is due to its social acceptance in the United States. One survey noted that 78 percent of women and 70 percent of men in the US strongly agreed with the statement: "It is okay for an unmarried female to have a child."[43] But a recent study using the NLSY97 dataset notes that having a child out of wedlock increases the risk of consistently poorer economic outcomes for the children, their mothers, and their unwed fathers and is an underlying factor in income inequality in the United States.[44] These data are another indication of the important role of intact and stable families in economic development.

Cultural Trends that Undermine Family Capital

Historically, marriage was deemed to be a primary goal for both men and women; for women it provided economic security and for men potential heirs. Moreover, marriage was valued since it generally enhanced one's social standing. Children were seen as assets by their parents because they provided labor and economic and social support for the family. Children were the designated resource to care for their parents as they aged. Furthermore, marriage and having children was encouraged by religious leaders. Clerics from the Christian tradition encouraged their parishioners to marry and "multiply and replenish the earth" as commanded by God in the Bible. Under these cultural conditions and practices, marriage and birth rates were high compared to such today.

Why have marriage and birth rates fallen so precipitously over the past several decades? The answer can be found in the attitudes and beliefs of many young people today regarding marriage and children. Many young people have witnessed the pain of the divorce of their parents, family members, or friends and have seen the economic and social challenges of marriages. In contrast, I grew up in a neighborhood where divorce was virtually unheard of, and we all assumed (probably incorrectly) that most people were happily married. So, through childhood and into early adulthood, I viewed marriage positively. Today, such a view is rare. And concerning children, I can paraphrase one of my single business students who said, "Children are a lot of hard work and they cost a lot to raise. In doing a cost-benefit analysis of having children, for many of us, the costs outweigh the benefits." (One recent survey from the United States shows that the cost of raising a child born in 2015 was $233,610.[45])

Where do these current beliefs about marriage and family come from? Many cultural icons of today—movie stars, politicians, writers, social activists, business leaders, and others whom young people today look to for guidance—tend to discount the importance of marriage and having children. For example, Oprah Winfrey has said that she didn't see marriage or children as part of her future. In one interview she said, "If I had kids, my kids would hate me. They would have ended up on the equivalent of the Oprah show talking about me" (*Hollywood Reporter* interview, 2013).[46] Other influential people have expressed similar views. Some of the following statements were intended to be humorous, but I believe they do reflect many people's views about family:

» "Marriage is the most expensive way for the average man to get laundry done" (actor Burt Reynolds, as reported in the *Huffington Post*).

» "We'd probably be excellent parents. But it's a human being and unless you think you have excellent skills and have a drive or yearning in you to do that, the amount of work that that is and responsibility—I wouldn't want to screw them up" (actress and talk show host Ellen DeGeneres in a *People* essay).

» "I don't like [the pressure] that people put on me, on women—that you've failed yourself as a female because you haven't procreated. I don't think it's fair. You may not have a child come out of your vagina, but that doesn't mean you aren't mothering—dogs, friends, friend's children" (actress Jennifer Aniston in an *Allure* interview).

» "Getting married is a lot like getting into a tub of hot water. After you get used to it, it ain't so hot" (Minnie Pearl of the Grand Ole Opry as reported by the *Huffington Post*).

» "I'm an old fashioned romantic. I believe in love and marriage—but not necessarily with the same person" (actor John Travolta as reported in the *Huffington Post*).

» "I work too much to be an appropriate parent. I feel like a bad mom to my dog some days because I'm just not here enough" (TV personality Rachael Ray in *People*).

» "It's like, 'Do you want to be an artist and a writer, or a wife and a lover?' With kids, your focus changes. I don't want to go to PTA meetings" (singer Stevie Nicks to *InStyle*).

» "Someone once asked me why women don't gamble as much as men do and I gave the commonsensical reply that we don't have as much money. That was a true but incomplete answer. In fact, women's total instinct for gambling is satisfied by marriage" (social activist Gloria Steinem as reported by the *Huffington Post*).

» "My wife and I were happy for twenty years. Then we met" (comedian Rodney Dangerfield as reported in the *Huffington Post*).

» "I don't have the marriage chip, and neither of us have the greatest examples of marriages in our families. Jen is the love of my life, and we've already been together four times longer than my parents were married" (actor and *Mad Men* star Jon Hamm in *Parade Magazine*, speaking about his break-up with Jennifer Westfeldt, his girlfriend of eighteen years).

These statements reflect a growing disillusionment with the institution of marriage and the role of a mother or father. The narrative around this disillusionment is found in the following set of beliefs:

» I don't think I would be a good wife/husband or mother/father, so marriage and parenthood are not for me.

» Marriage is risky since many marriages fail; furthermore, marriage can inflict pain and can be expensive both psychologically and financially.

» Raising children is time consuming, costly, and boring.

» Having a career is more important than marriage and children. Raising children is not as valued in society as your career outside the home.

» Cohabiting and relationships outside of marriage can be as meaningful, if not more meaningful, than a marriage relationship. And if I were to have a child as the result of such a relationship, I'd have someone to love and who loves me—somehow things would work out.

These five beliefs seem to be increasingly accepted in the United States and many other countries and significantly drive the declining marriage and birth rates and the rise of cohabitation and out-of-wedlock births. Furthermore, these beliefs are largely based on the assumption that your personal needs and happiness should drive decisions around marriage and children.

In addition to these cultural trends, research has described millennials as being more individualistic and narcissistic than prior generations;[47] lacking empathy[48] and teamwork skills;[49] unaccepting of personal responsibility for failure;[50] and being emotionally needy, constantly needing praise and validation.[51] Although exceptions to this psychological profile of millennials certainly exist, the research suggests a perfect storm as these individuals navigate cultures that support the values of individualism, self-absorption, and personal accomplishment rather than focusing on others—thus leading to a lack of interest in marriage and having children. We know that behavior is a function of individuals with certain values interacting with the cultural values that surround them. And, of course, a recursive, self-reinforcing, dynamic occurs: the culture influences individuals to adopt certain values, and individuals who adopt those values become role models of those values for the broader society.

This individualism is behind the relatively recent phenomenon of "sologamy"—marrying yourself. Although the ceremony carries no legal weight, for some it does have symbolic significance. The BBC, in reporting a story on a sologamous marriage in Italy, interviewed the woman, Laura Mesi, who married herself. She said: "I firmly believe that each of us must first of all love ourselves. You can have a fairy tale even without the prince."[52] The BBC noted that such "marriages" are believed to have initially begun in 1993, and while not large in number, seem to be growing in popularity.

Figure 2.1 presents a visual representation of the trends from 1950 to the projected year 2020. To put these trends in the same figure we needed to calculate them in terms of percentages. In addition to the five trends—marriage rates (percent over age fifteen who are married), divorce rates (percent over age fifteen who have been divorced), birth rates (percent of women over forty who are childless), cohabitation rates (percent who are cohabiting), and out-of-wedlock birth rates (percent of out-of-wedlock births)—I have added an additional dimension, that of "single-parent homes with children under eighteen," which is typically a function of divorce or out-of-wedlock births. Households with only one parent have increased in the United States from under 10 percent in 1950 to over 30 percent today.

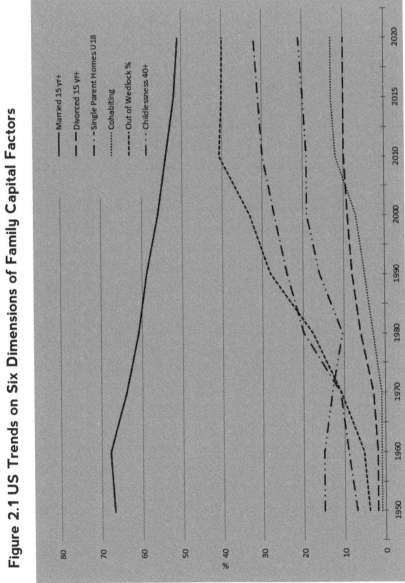

Figure 2.1 US Trends on Six Dimensions of Family Capital Factors

The trends described in figure 2.1 do not necessarily apply to all countries and cultures. But, in general, the trends of other countries are similar.

Comparing Racial Groups in the United States

Asian Americans, at 12 percent self-employment, are better able to succeed in starting and growing new businesses. Data from various sources offer explanations as to why. Recent data from the Survey of Minority-Owned Business Enterprises (SMOBE), the Survey of Business Owners (SBO), the Survey of Characteristics of Business Owners (CBO), and the Current Population Survey (CPS) provide important insights concerning family demographics and entrepreneurial activity within certain racial and ethnic groups in the United States. Using data from these sources, Robert Fairlie and Alicia Robb summarize the basic findings of their study related to business ownership and firm outcomes for whites, Asian Americans, Hispanics, and African Americans:[53]

> » African Americans and Hispanics are much less likely to own a business than are whites or Asian Americans. CPS data indicate that 12 percent of Asian American workers, 11 percent of white workers, 7 percent of Hispanic workers, and only 5 percent of black workers own their own business.
> » Asian American-owned firms "clearly have the strongest performance among all major racial and ethnic groups." Asian American-owned firms are 16 percent less likely to close, 21 percent more likely to have profits of at least $10,000, and 27 percent more likely to hire employees; moreover, they have mean sales 60 percent higher than firms owned by whites.
> » African American-owned companies have lower sales and profits, hire fewer people, and have higher closure rates than white-owned firms. Hispanic firms also have lower sales and hire fewer employees than white-owned firms.[54]

The trends in terms of marriage, cohabitation, divorce, birth rates, and out-of-wedlock birth rates are affecting access to family capital in each of these groups. Table 2.1 (opposite) summarizes these differences. The data come from a variety of sources at different times, given that finding accurate family data based on race is fairly difficult. Most of the data in table 2.1 are from several years ago when I started studying the impact of race on self-employment. However, 2016–2017 statistics from the US Census and Bureau of Labor Statistics indicate that the differences between the racial groups along these five dimensions have remained fairly stable over time.[55]

It is not surprising, given our theory linking family capital to entrepreneurial activity, that Asian Americans have historically had high rates of self-employment and create larger and more successful businesses than do the self-employed in the other racial/ethnic groups in the United States. Asian Americans have the second highest marriage rate (71.6 percent), the second highest birth rate (17.2 percent), and the lowest rates of divorce (4.9 percent), out-of-wedlock births (26 per 1,000), and cohabitation (5 percent). In short, Asian Americans have each of the five factors affecting family capital going in the "right" direction for them. In comparison, African Americans have the lowest marriage rate (53.9 percent), are third in birth rate (16.9 per 1,000), are second in out-of-wedlock births (72 per 1,000) and have the highest divorce (11.5 percent) and cohabitation (17 percent) rates. Whites are fairly similar to Asian Americans but are more likely to cohabit and be divorced. Hispanics did well in comparison to the other groups on dimensions such as divorce rate and cohabitation, but they have an extremely high number of out-of-wedlock births (106 per 1,000). While these data obviously don't tell the whole picture of why certain groups are more entrepreneurial than others, they do suggest that those individuals with more stable families with access to family capital will be more likely to launch a business and make it successful over time. Economist and Nobel laureate Gary Becker supports this notion that the family is important to economic development when he writes, "The family is still crucial to a well-functioning economy

Table 2.1: Racial/Ethnic Groups in the United States in Regards to
Marriage, Cohabitation, Divorce, Birth Rate, and Out-of-Wedlock Births

	% Ever Married[1]	% Cohabitating[2]	% Divorced[3]	Birth Rate[4]	Out-of-Wedlock Births[5]	%Self-employed[6]
Asians	71.6	5.0	4.9	17.2	26	12
Whites	72.5	8.2	10.8	13.7	32	11
Hispanics	64.0	12.2	7.8	23.4	106	7
Blacks	53.9	17.0	11.5	16.9	72	5

and society, and I believe—in the long run—that those economies that
will advance most rapidly will tend to have strong family structures."[56]

Besides changes in American families over the years, institutional
racism has also played a role in inhibiting minority groups, particularly African Americans, from creating new enterprises and generating

wealth. In the case of African Americans, the disadvantages created by slavery are inextricably connected to the destruction of their family capital. The ability of slave owners to buy and sell family members disrupted family ties. Although informal "marriages" were performed, the law forbade slaves from formally marrying. Moreover, slavery obliterated African Americans' sense of identity in a tribe or clan, which was an integral part of family life in Africa. This further undermined family social capital and stymied the transfer of family capital across generations. Slavery made it difficult for African Americans to even identify themselves as part of a family and thus they often took their master's surname to provide them with some connection to a family, albeit not their own. African Americans had few familial resources to help themselves and their loved ones and thus, out of necessity, became dependent upon the slave owners, the government, or other institutions—curbing their ability to become self-reliant. The net effect on the African American community was a lack of resources to start and grow businesses and provide for their families. Thus, the disruption of family relationships to keep minority groups in a subservient position has played an important role in racism in America. The complete story of slavery and racism and its impact on families and family capital is too long and complex to be considered here, but its recognition is important. Moreover, current family patterns within the African American community, some of which may be a function of its history, continue to make it difficult for African Americans to generate family capital.

Worldwide Trends Regarding the Family

The trends in the United States regarding marriage, cohabitation, fertility rates, divorce, and out-of-wedlock births tend to mirror global trends. Marriage rates are declining in much of the industrialized world. In fact, despite its recent decline in marriage, the United States generally leads the developed world in marriage rates—9.8 per 1,000 people per year. Other selected countries' marriage rates per 1,000 are as follows: Russia, 8.9; Portugal, 7.3; Israel, 7; New Zealand, 7; Australia, 6.9; Denmark, 6.1; Greece, 5.8; Japan, 5.8; Italy, 5.4; France, 5.1; Finland, 4.8; and Sweden, 4.7.[57]

The decline in birth rates is similar. For example, various studies project that given current birth rates Europe will have approximately forty to one hundred million fewer people by 2050.[58]

Here's a sampling of fertility rates in developed countries: France, 2.08; United Kingdom, 1.91; Chile, 1.87; Australia, 1.77; Russia, 1.61; Canada, 1.59; China, 1.55; Italy, 1.40; Ukraine, 1.29; Czech Republic, 1.27; Taiwan, 1.10; and Singapore, 0.78.[59] Eleven countries with the highest birth rates are in Africa; however, poor nutrition and disease (particularly AIDS) have led to a significant number of single-parent families there, in addition to a significant number of orphans. In South Africa alone 5.6 million people are infected by AIDS, with 310,000 dying of the disease each year.[60] AIDS has left 11 million orphan children in sub-Saharan Africa.[61]

Mara Hvistendahl's book *Unnatural Selection*[62] and Valerie Hudson's and Andrea den Boer's book, *Bare Branches*,[63] highlight a very troubling fact—due to selective abortions and female infanticide in Asia (mostly in India and China), there are well over one hundred million fewer women than men in Asia. Thus, many young men in Asia will not be able to find a mate who could provide them with family capital or help them found and perpetuate a business.

Divorce, while increasingly common, varies dramatically across the world. The highest divorce rates are in Europe (e.g., Sweden, 54.9 percent), Australia (46 percent), the United States (45.8 percent) and Russia (43.3 percent), while divorce rates in the Middle East (e.g., Turkey, 6 percent) and Asia (e.g., India, 1.1 percent) are much lower.[64] Higher divorce rates can result in fewer family businesses and fewer family firms passed to the next generation.

Much like fertility rates, out-of-wedlock births vary dramatically by country. In Japan, for example, only 2 percent of all births are out-of-wedlock. Other countries in Asia (e.g., Korea) also have a low rate. However, in countries elsewhere, particularly in Europe, the rates are significantly higher: Italy, 30 percent; Ireland, 35 percent; Netherlands, 50 percent; Sweden, 55 percent; Iceland, 66 percent. In South America, Colombia is at a staggering 84 percent.[65] Furthermore, out-of-wedlock birth rates have increased dramatically over the past decades in certain countries. For example, in 1970 the out-of-wedlock birth rate in the Netherlands was less than 3 percent but had increased to about 50 percent by 2016.[66]

Worldwide trends regarding the family suggest that families in Asia are generally more stable than those in the West—they have more marriages, fewer divorces, and fewer out-of-wedlock births. However, family size and fewer women available for marriage could negatively affect Asian family capital in the future. In North America, Europe, and Australia, family size, divorce, marriage, and out-of-wedlock birth rates continue to undermine familial capital. In Africa and South America, the picture is less clear. Birth rates in Africa and South America are relatively high compared to other continents, but out-of-wedlock births, divorce, and marriage rates are problematic for family capital in many countries on these continents.

So do these family trends affect entrepreneurial activity in the various countries worldwide? Data from the Global Entrepreneurship Monitor (GEM) suggest a connection.[67] On a regular basis, GEM researchers gather data about entrepreneurship intentions and business start-up rates worldwide. Comparing start-up rates and entrepreneurial activity across nations is very difficult because of differences in political systems, economies, cultures, and so forth. However, I decided to do a gross comparison of industrialized countries using the five dimensions related to family capital—marriage, divorce, cohabitation, fertility, and out-of-wedlock births—to see if there might be some connection between these factors and new business ownership rates.[68] The countries included in the panel are Australia, Canada, China, France, Germany, Italy, Japan, Russia, Sweden, Taiwan, the United Kingdom, and the United States (see table 2.2).

As shown in the table, China has the highest new business ownership rate, partly due to the entrepreneurial spirit among the Chinese

Table 2.2: Family Patterns in Industrialized Countries and New Business Ownership

	Marriage Rate %[1]	Total Fertility Rate[2]	Crude Divorce Rate[3]	Cohabitation Rate %[4]	Out-of-Wedlock Birth Rate %[5]	New Business Ownership Rate[6]
Australia	43%	1.9	2.1	14%	33%	5.7
Canada	43%	1.7	2.2	19%	33%	5.6
China	~50%	1.7	1.8	1%	~2%	10.2
France	39%	2.0	1.9	26%	57%	1.7
Germany	42%	1.4	2.1	11%	35%	2.3
Italy	54%	1.5	0.9	2%	27%	1.3
Japan	69%	1.4	1.8	2%	2%	1.3
Russia	50%	1.5	4.5	9%	25%	2.4
Sweden	27%	1.9	2.8	24%	54%	1.9
Taiwan	49%	1.1	2.3	2%	4%	4.1
United Kingdom	47%	1.9	2.1	9%	48%	4.5
United States	49%	2.0	2.8	15%	41%	4.3

~Estimates based on best data available from China.

and their recent changes to a more capitalist economy. But they also have more stable families compared to the other industrialized nations, with high marriage rates, relatively low divorce rates, and very low cohabitation and out-of-wedlock birth rates. The only problematic area for the Chinese is the low birth rate, which is being partly addressed by the easing of the one-child policy in China. In contrast, some of the European countries listed in table 2.2 such as France and Sweden have high out-of-wedlock birth rates (57 and 54 percent, respectively) and high cohabitation rates (26 and 24 percent). Both have relatively low marriage rates (39 and 27 percent). New business ownership rates in those countries are some of the lowest in the world at 1.7 and 1.9 percent. Two European countries seemingly somewhat better than France and Sweden along the five family capital dimensions are Germany and Russia, which have a 2.3 and a 2.4 new business ownership rate, respectively. Russia has a high marriage rate but also a high divorce rate—one of the highest in the world—while Germany has lower cohabitation and out-of-wedlock birth rates than do France and Sweden. Italy and Japan, on the other hand, have lower new business ownership rates than the other countries, but seem to have a somewhat more stable family structure (lower cohabitation and lower out-of-wedlock births) than some other countries, although both have very low fertility rates. Thus, there is clearly more to the story of entrepreneurship in Italy and Japan than is shown by these data.

The United States, the United Kingdom, Canada, and Australia had higher new business ownership rates than Europe did. In general, these countries had relatively low cohabitation rates, modest divorce rates (with the exception of the US), and marriage rates ranging from 43 to 49 percent, but somewhat high out-of-wedlock birth rates (ranging from 33 to 48 percent). Thus these countries have both strengths and weaknesses in family capital. Taiwan appears to have stable families and a fairly robust new business ownership rate (4.1 percent)—but it has one of the lowest fertility rates in the world (1.1 per 1,000), which would clearly undermine family capital.

Table 2.3 Family Demographics from Selected Latin American Countries

	Marriage Rate %[1]	Total Fertility Rate[2]	Crude Divorce Rate[3]	Cohabitation Rate %[4]	Out-of-Wedlock Birth Rate %[5]
Brazil	35%	1.8	0.9	24%	66%
Chile	29%	1.8	3.0	20%	71%
Colombia	20%	2.3	0.2	35%	84%
Mexico	63%	2.2	0.9	10%	55%

In tables 2.3 and 2.4 we have a description of the five dimensions affecting family capital for the Latin American countries of Brazil, Chile, Colombia, and Mexico and the African countries of Ethiopia, Nigeria, South Africa, and Tanzania. Data on business start-up are much less trustworthy in these countries since many start-ups are out of necessity and aren't what would be called true entrepreneurial ventures. Nevertheless, Latin America and Africa have high poverty rates and poor economic growth compared to the rest of the world. The poverty implies fairly low access to family capital to launch a new business or provide a safety net for family members when times are difficult.

The data from table 2.3 on Latin America exposes some of the problems. First, there is a very high out-of-wedlock birth rate ranging from a high of 84 percent in Colombia to 55 percent in Mexico. Marriage rates, with the exception of Mexico, are also quite low, with modest cohabitation rates ranging from 10 percent in Mexico to 35 percent in Colombia. Fertility rates are modest as are divorce rates, with the exception of Chile. In many Latin American countries divorce is costly so leaving one's spouse without getting a divorce is common. Hence, we often find a higher cohabitation rate in these countries versus other countries where divorce is easy to obtain. For those who separate from their spouse and cannot legally marry someone else without a divorce, a common law/cohabiting relationship may seem their only option. Thus, the state of families and family capital in Latin America suggests a difficult road ahead to stimulate economic activity and move people out of poverty.

The story of families in sub-Saharan Africa is fairly complex, because not only is family structure being torn apart from negative political and social conditions but also civil wars, AIDS, and other diseases have left millions of children as orphans—making access to family capital virtually impossible for them. In the four countries listed, you will note the higher birth rates versus Latin America and the industrialized nations. Nigeria, at 6.0 children per woman, has one of the highest birth-rates in the world but also has a high divorce rate. South Africa, on the other hand, has a low marriage rate compared to the other countries and thus, not surprisingly, a higher cohabitation and out-of-wedlock birth rate. The history of slavery and colonialism in Africa along with the emergence of brutal dictators and civil wars have clearly disrupted family structures and family capital and stymied economic development in African nations.

Table 2.4 Family Structure in Sub-Saharan Africa (selected countries)

	Marriage Rate %[1]	Total Fertility Rate[2]	Crude Divorce Rate[3]	Cohabitation Rate %[4]	Out-of-Wedlock Birth Rate %[5]
Ethiopia	63%	4.5	2.2	4%	11%
Nigeria	48%	6.0	5.0	3%	7%
South Africa	26%	2.4	.7	12%	63%
Tanzania	60%	2.4	2.1	7%	29%

A Country with a Family Capital Crisis: The Case of Swaziland (or eSwatini)

While studying the challenges countries have in developing family capital, I became interested in the special problems facing countries in sub-Saharan Africa. In the spring of 2017, I traveled to Africa with Faculty Development in International Business (FDIB), a program for business school academics sponsored by the US government, visiting South Africa, Zambia, Zimbabwe, Botswana, and Swaziland.[69] My five days in Swaziland were particularly interesting from a family capital perspective given the country's challenges. I gathered information about Swazi society from local Swazi business leaders, government representatives, and Swazi academics, as well as US diplomats stationed there.

Swaziland is a small country of about 1.4 million people located at the east end of southern Africa, bordered by South Africa on the north, south, and west, and by Mozambique on the east. The country is the homeland of the Swazi tribe and has been ruled by kings for many generations. The minimal industry mainly relates to sugarcane, tourism, and handicrafts, but the country manufactures and distributes Coca-Cola concentrate for all of southern Africa. (Coca-Cola relocated its plant to Swaziland from South Africa many years ago when companies began boycotting South Africa due to apartheid.) Subsistence farming is the dominant practice in Swaziland, which provides little income for Swazis; therefore, the government depends heavily on customs duties from the Southern African Customs Union (SACU) and worker remittances from Swazis who have left Swaziland to find work in other countries, primarily South Africa.

In terms of family capital, the Swazi culture discourages safe-sex practices such as condom use and monogamous marriages, and it encourages a man to impregnate as many women as possible. Moreover, significant social stigma is attached to anyone with a sexually transmitted disease (primarily HIV/AIDS), which discourages people from being tested and seeking treatment. These beliefs and practices have led to Swaziland having the highest incidence of HIV/ AIDS in the world (31 percent of the population), a life expectancy of 49 years, low marriage rates, high out-of-wedlock birth rates, many orphans (one in four children, primarily due to AIDS), and a low percentage (22 percent) of children growing up in two-parent families. However, polygamy is found among the well-to-do in Swazi society.

The king and the royal family also play a role in shaping Swazi promiscuity and marriage instability. The previous king, Sobhuza II, was born in 1899 and was crowned as an infant after his father died. Sobhuza II had 70 wives and 210 children (and thousands of grandchildren and great grandchildren). One of the king's practices was to have virgins (typically in their teens) paraded before him periodically so that he could choose one of them as a future wife. However, once chosen to be a future wife, the girl would need to be impregnated by Sobhuza II before becoming eligible for marriage to the king. This practice has continued with the current king, Mswati III, who has 15 wives (although the actual total is debatable). Mswati III's mother had not been officially married to Sobhuza II before he died, so to legitimate Mswati III's birth and status a marriage ceremony was performed for Mswati's mother and Sobhuza II's corpse—an unusual marriage ceremony to say the least. The king rules Swaziland by edict (although the country has a nominal constitution) and he has a $200 million trust fund of which about $61 million is used each year to support his family. (The king and the principal wives all have elaborate palaces.) As for the rest of the country, 63 percent of Swazis live in poverty and 29 percent live in extreme poverty, meaning they live on less than one dollar per day.

Swaziland has beautiful scenery and friendly people, but the outcomes associated with the breakdown of the family in Swaziland are unmistakable: little entrepreneurial activity, high unemployment (about 40 percent), a high poverty rate (63 percent), and a national health crisis associated with sexually transmitted diseases.

Although Swaziland is an extreme case, data from other countries in Africa, South America, and other parts of the world suggest that family capital is increasingly scarce. This does not bode well for the economic health and stability of many countries throughout the world.

Chapter Takeaways

» Cultural narratives in the United States regarding marriage and children are having a negative impact on family capital.

» Family capital, or the lack of it, affects entrepreneurial activity worldwide.

» Family capital among nations, although difficult to ascertain, can be shown using rudimentary data.

» Generally, worldwide trends do not bode well for family capital.

Notes

1. Paul C. Rosenblatt et al., *The Family in Business* (San Francisco: Jossey-Bass, 1985).

2. Robert W. Fairlie and Alicia M. Robb, *Race and Entrepreneurial Success* (Cambridge: MIT Press, 2008).

3. Sanders, J., & Nee, V. 1996. "Social Capital, Human Capital, and Immigrant Self-Employment: The Family As Social Capital and the Value of Human Capital," *American Sociological Review* 61 no. 2 (1996): 240–41.

4. Fairlie and Robb, *Race and Entrepreneurial Success*.

5. Roger Peay and W. Gibb Dyer Jr., "Power Orientations of Entrepreneurs and Succession Planning," *Journal of Small Business Management* 27 no. 1 (1989): 47–52.

6. *Estimated Median Age at First Marriage, by Sex: 1890 to the Present* prepared by the United States Census Bureau, https://www.census.gov/data/tables/time-series/demo/families/marital.html.

7. *Marital Status of the Population 15 Years and Over, by Sex, Race and Hispanic Orgin: 1950 to Present* prepared by the United States Census Bureau, https://www.census.gov/data/tables/time-series/demo/families/marital.html.

8. Kim Parker and Renee Stepler, "As US Marriage Rate Hovers at 50%, Education Gap in Marital Status Widens," *Pew Research Center*, http://www.pewresearch.org/fact-tank/2017/09/14/as-u-s-marriage-rate-hovers-at-50-education-gap-in-marital-status-widens.

9. Howard E. Aldrich and Jennifer E. Cliff, "The Pervasive Effects of Family on Entrepreneurship: Toward a Family Embeddedness Perspective," *Journal of Business Venturing* 18 (2003): 581.

10. Howard E. Aldrich and Nancy Langton, "Human Resource Management and Organizational Life Cycles," *Frontiers of Entrepreneurship Research* (1997): 349–357.

11. Ivan Light and Steven J. Gold, "Ethnic Economies and Social Policy," *Research in Social Movement, Conflict and Change* 22 (2000): 87.

12. Light and Gold, "Ethnic Economies and Social Policy," 87.

13. Lloyd Steier and Royston Greenwood, "Entrepreneurship and the Evolution of Angel Financial Networks," *Organization Studies* 21 (2000): 163–92.

14. Fairlie and Robb, *Race and Entrepreneurial Success*, 92.

15. Lyman Stone, "American Fertility Is Falling Short of What Women Want," *New York Times*, February 13, 2018.

16. James S. Coleman, "Social Capital in the Creation of Human Capital," *American Journal of Sociology* 94 (1988): S95–S120.

17. Fairlie and Robb, *Race and Entrepreneurial Success*, 187.

18. P. R. Amato, "The Impact of Family Formation Change on the Cognitive, Social and Emotional Well-Being of the Next Generation," *Future of Children* 15 no. 2 (2005): 77.

19. Ibid., 77.

20. Jeremy Arkes, "The Temporal Effects of Parental Divorce on Youth Substance Use," *Substance Use & Misuse* 48 no. 3 (2013): 290–97, https://www.ncbi.nlm.nih.gov/pubmed/23363082.

21. *Overdose Death Rates* prepared by the National Institute on Drug Abuse, https://www.drugabuse.gov/related-topics/trends-statistics/overdose-death-rates.

22. Amato, "The Impact of Family Formation Change on the Cognitive, Social and Emotional Well-Being of the Next Generation," 75–96.

23. Bradford Wilcox et al., "When Marriage Disappears: The Retreat from Marriage in Middle America," *State of Our Unions* (2010).

24. Linda J. Waite, "Does Marriage Matter?" *Demography* 32 no. 4 (1995): 483–507.

25. Scott M. Stanley, Sarah W. Whitton, and Howard J. Markman, "Maybe I do: Interpersonal Commitment and Premarital or Nonmarital Cohabitation," *Journal of Family Issues* 25 (2004): 496–519.

26. Susan L. Brown, Wendy D. Manning, and Krista K. Payne, "Relationship Quality Among Cohabiting Versus Married Couples," *National Center for Family & Marriage Research* 14 no. 3 (2014).

27. Sanders Korenman and David Neumark, "Marriage, Motherhood, and Wages," *Journal of Human Resources* 27 no. 2 (1990): 233–255.

28. Lee A. Lillard and Linda J. Waite, "Till Death Do Us Part: Marital Disruption and Mortality," *American Journal of Sociology* 100 no. 5 (1995): 1131–56.

29. Paul R. Amato and Alan Booth, *A Generation at Risk: Growing Up in an Era of Family Upheaval* (Cambridge, MA: Harvard University Press, 2000).

30. Linda J. Waite, "Social science finds: 'Marriage matters'," *Responsive Community* 6 (1996): 26–35.

31. Jeffrey H. Larson, 2001. "The Verdict on Cohabitation Vs. Marriage," *Marriage & Families* 4 no. 3 (2001), http://marriageandfamilies.byu.edu/issues/2001/January/cohabitation.htm.

32. Susan L. Brown, "Family Structure and Child Well-Being: The Significance of Parental Cohabitation, *Journal of Marriage and the Family* 66 (2004): 351–67.

33. Robert Whelan, *Broken Homes and Battered Children: A Study of the Relationship Between Child Abuse and Family Type* (London: Family Education Trust, 1994).

34. Elizabeth H. Pleck, *Not Just Roommates: Cohabitation After the Sexual Revolution* (Chicago: University of Chicago Press, 2012).

35. Daniel T. Lichter, Richard N. Turner, and Sharon Sassler, "National Estimates of the Rise in Serial Cohabitation," *Social Science Research* 39 no. 5 (2010): 754–65.

36. *National Survey of Family Growth* prepared by the U.S. Department of Health & Human Services, https://www.cdc.gov/nchs/nsfg/key_statistics/c.htm#currentcohab.

37. Alfred Demaris and Vaninadha Rao, "Premarital Cohabitation and Subsequent Marital Stability in the United States: A Reassessment," *Journal of Marriage and the Family* 54 no. 1 (1992): 178–90.

Susan L. Brown, Wendy D. Manning, and Krista K. Payne, "Relationship Quality Among Cohabiting Versus Married Couples," *Journal of Family Issues* 38 no. 12 (2014): 1730–1753.

38. L. L. Bumpass, T. C. Martin, and J. A. Sweet, "The Impact of Family Background and Early Marital Factors on Marital Disruption," *Journal of Family Issues* 12 no. 1 (1991): 22–42.

Brown, Manning, and Payne, "Relationship Quality Among Cohabiting Versus Married Couples," 1730–53.

39. Ibid.

40. Marcia Carlson, Sara McLanahan, and Paula England, "Union Formation and Dissolution in Fragile Families," *Center for Research on Child Wellbeing* 41 no. 2 (2004): 237–61.

41. Bradford Wilcox et al., "When Marriage Disappears: The Retreat from Marriage in Middle America."

42. *Recent Declines in Nonmarital Childbearing in the United States* prepared by the Centers for Disease Control and Prevention, https://www.cdc.gov/nchs/data/databriefs/db162.htm.

43. Andrew Cherlin, David C. Ribar, and Suzumi Yasutake, "Nonmarital First Births, Marriage, and Income Inequality," *American Sociological Review* 81 no. 4 (2016): 749–70.

44. Ibid., 749–70.

45. Kathryn Vasel, "The Cost of the American Dream," *CNN Money,* January 9, 2017, http://money.cnn.com/2017/01/09/pf/cost-of-raising-a-child-2015/index.html.

46. The quotes from the various celebrities can be found in the following two sources:

"Celebrity Marriage: Craziest Stuff Stars Say About Marriage," *Life,* July 20, 2012, http://www.huffingtonpost.com/entry/celebrity-marriage_n_1688174.html?slideshow=true#gallery/239768/17.

"23 Celebrities Reveal How They Feel About Not Having Kids," *Elle,* September 14, 2017, http://www.elle.com/culture/celebrities/a35545/celebrities-not-having-kids-quotes.

47. Jean M. Twenge, W. Keith Campbell, and Elise C. Freeman, "Generational Differences in Young Adults' Life Goals, Concern for Others and Civic Orientation, 1966–2009," *Journal of Personality and Social Psychology* 102 no. 5 (2012): 1045–62.

48. Sara H. Konrath, Edward H. O'Brien, and Courtney Hsing, "Changes in Dispositional Empathy in American College Students Over Time: A Metal Analysis," *Personality and Social Psychology Review* 15 no. 1 (2011): 180–98.

49. Twenge, Campbell, and Freeman, "Generational Differences in Young Adults' Life Goals, Concern for Others and Civic Orientation, 1966–2009," 1045–62.

50. J. M. Twenge, L. Zhang, and C. Im, "It's Beyond My Control: A Crosstemporal Meta-Analysis of Increasing Externality in Locus of Control, 1960–2002." *Personality and Social Psychology Review* 8 no. 3 (2004): 308–19.

51. Martha Crumpacker and Jill M. Crumpacker, "Succession Planning and Generational Stereotypes: Should HR Consider Age-Based Values and Attitudes a Relevant Factor or a Passing Fad?" *Public Personnel Management* 36 no. 4 (2007): 349–69.

52. "Italy Woman Marries Herself in 'Fairytale without Prince'," *BBC News,* September 27, 2017, http://www.bbc.com/news/world-europe-41413297.

53. Fairlie and Robb, *Race and Entrepreneurial Success.*

54. Ibid., 10.

55. Joyce A. Marlin et al., "Births: Final Data for 2016," National Vital Statistics Reports 67 no. 1 (2018).

56. Gary Becker, "Human Capital," *Universidad de Montevideo,* http://www.um.edu.uy/docs/revistafcee/2002/humancapitalBecker.pdf, p. 2.

57. *United Nations Monthly Bulletin of Statistics, April 2001* prepared by the Department of Economic and Social Affairs.

58. https://www.ft.com/content/d54e4fe8-3269-11e8-b5bf-23cb17fd1498

59. *World Factbook 2012* prepared by the Central Intelligence Agency.

60. *World Factbook 2011* prepared by the Central Intelligence Agency.

61. https://www.avert.org/professionals/hiv-social-issues/key-affected-populations/children

62. Mara Hvistendahl, *Unnatural Selection: Choosing Boys Over Girls and the Consequences of a World Full of Men* (New York: Public Affairs, 2012).

63. Valerie M. Hudson and Andrea M. den Boer, *Bare Branches: The Security Implications of Asia's Surplus Male Population* (Cambridge, MA: MIT Press, 2004).

64. *World Divorce Statistics* prepared by *Divorce Magazine,* October 14, 2014, www.divorce-mag.com/statistics/statsWorld.shtml.

65. "Share of Births Outside of Marriage," *Organization for Economic Cooperation and Development* (2018), https://www.oecd.org/els/family/SF_2_4_Share_births_outside_marriage.pdf.

66. Ibid.

67. D. Kelley, S. Singer, and M. Harrington, *Global Entrepreneurship Monitor: 2011.*

68. Data on marriage, divorce, fertility, cohabitation, and out-of-wedlock births come from the following sources: World Family Map, 1998–2013; United Nations World Marriage Data; *Sustainable Demographic Dividend* prepared by the Social Trends Institue—Mexico, 2006 and Chile, 2010; United Nations Statistical Division.

69. Information about Swaziland was gathered from the following sources: *World Factbook 2015* prepared by the Central Intelligence Agency; Mindy E. Scott et al., "World Family Map 2015," *Institute for Family Studies,* http://worldfamilymap.ifstudies.org/2015; *Statistics* prepared by Unicef, www.unicef.org/infobycountry/swaziland_statistics.html; Ambassador Lisa Peterson and the U.S. embassy staff in Swaziland, May 18, 2017; and Robert Rolfe, Professor, University of South Carolina.

Figure 2.1

Historical Marital Status Tables prepared by the United States Census Bureau, https://www.census.gov/data/tables/time-series/demo/families/marital.html.

Historical Families Tables prepared by the United States Census Bureau, https://www.census.gov/data/tables/time-series/demo/families/families.html.

Casey E. Copen et al., "First Marriages in the United States: Data From the 2006–2010 National Survey of Family Growth," National Health Statistics Reports 49 (2012), https://www.cdc.gov/nchs/data/nhsr/nhsr049.pdf and https://www.cdc.gov/nchs/nsfg/key_statistics/c.htm#chabitation (This data was the least available so years 1950-1970 were extrapolated at 1% from the data).

National Vital Statistics Reports, https://www.cdc.gov/nchs/data/statab/t991x17.pdf, https://www.cdc.gov/nchs/data/nvsr/nvsr65/nvsr65_03.pdf, and https://www.cdc.gov/nchs/data/nvsr/nvsr62/nvsr62_09.pdf.

Gretchen Livingston and D'Vera Cohn, "Childlessness Up Among All Women; Down Among Women with Advanced Degrees," Pew Research Center, June 25, 2010, http://www.pewsocialtrends.org/2010/06/25/childlessness-up-among-all-women-down-among-women-with-advanced-degrees.

"The Rise of Childlessness," *The Economist,* July 27, 2017, https://www.economist.com/news/international/21725553-more-adults-are-not-having-children-much-less-worrying-it-appears-rise.

Table 2.1

1. US Census, 2009 (Average of Data on Men and Women).

2. Tivia Simmons and Martin O'Connell, "Married-Couple and Unmarried-Partner Households: 2000." Census 2000 Special Reports. U.S. Census Bureau 2003. Reports number of children born per 1000 women of child-bearing age.

3. US Census 5-Year community study, Jan. 1, 2005–Dec. 31, 2009.

4. National Vital Statistics Reports for 2007, Vo. 58, No. 4.

5. Stephanie J. Ventura, Changing Patterns of Nonmarital Childbearing in the United States, NCHS Data Brief, no. 18, May 2009. Reports number of births per 1000 non-married women of childbearing age.

6. Fairlie and Robb, 2008.

Table 2.2

1. Percentage of married adults of reproductive age (18–49).

2. Number of children who would be born per woman if she lived to the end of her childbearing years and bore children at each age in accordance with prevailing age-specific fertility rates.

3. Total number of divorces per 1,000 population.

4. Percentage of cohabitating adults of reproductive age (18–49).

5. Percentage of all live births to unmarried women.

6. Percentage of individuals aged 18–64 who are currently an owner-manager of a new business, i.e., owning and managing a running business that has paid salaries, wages, or any other payments to the owners for more than 3 months but not more than 42 months.

Table 2.3

1. Percentage of married adults of reproductive age (18–49).

2. Number of children who would be born per woman if she lived to the end of her childbearing years and bore children at each age in accordance with prevailing age-specific fertility rates.

3. Total number of divorces per 1,000 population.

4. Percentage of cohabiting adults of reproductive age (18–49).

5. Percentage of all live births to unmarried women.

Table 2.4

1. Percentage of married adults of reproductive age (18–49).

2. Number of children who would be born per woman if she lived to the end of her childbearing years and bore children at each age in accordance with prevailing age-specific fertility rates.

3. Total number of divorces per 1,000 population.

4. Percentage of cohabitating adults of reproductive age (18–49).

5. Percentage of all live births to unmarried women.

You don't choose your family. They are God's gift to you, as you are to them.

Desmond Tutu, Nobel Peace Prize winner

CHAPTER 3

THE IMPACT OF FAMILY STRUCTURE ON FAMILY CAPITAL

F amily structure provides the framework upon which family capital is built. The various structures directly affect the stability of family relationships and the size of the family network, both of which allow family capital to be developed, maintained, and accessed. In this chapter I will describe the different family structures, their prevalence, and their ability to generate and maintain family capital.

Types of Family Structures

The National Health Interview Survey (NHIS),[1] conducted in the United States by the National Center for Health Statistics (NCHS), identifies family structures, whose distribution in the United States can be found in table 3.1.

Table 3.1 Households with Children Below Age Eighteen in the United States (2001–2007)

Family Structure	All	Non-Hispanic Black	Hispanic
Nuclear	48.4%	20.5%	41.0%
Extended	19.0%	22.4%	27.6%
Blended	8.7%	8.0%	7.1%
Cohabiting	3.1%	3.7%	3.0%
Single mom	13.6%	32.0%	13.5%
Single dad	1.7%	2.0%	0.9%
Single adult with one or more children	1.0%	3.5%	0.9%
Unmarried biological or adoptive	1.5%	1.7%	2.4%
Other	3.1%	6.3%	3.8%

A *nuclear family* consists of one or more children living with two parents who are married to one another and are each a biological or adoptive parent to all children in the family. In the United States, slightly less than half (48 percent) of all families would be classified as nuclear families; however this varies dramatically by race. For example, only 20.5 percent of African American children are in a nuclear family (a lower percentage than the children in Swaziland), while 41 percent of Hispanic children are in nuclear families and 57 percent of white children live with both parents.

An *extended family* consists of one or more children living with at least one biological or adoptive parent and a related nonparent adult (e.g., grandparent, adult sibling). Any of the other described family types that contain an adult son or daughter are categorized as an extended family as well. Given this definition by the NHIS, 19 percent of families in the United States are extended families and the percentages differ significantly by racial group: 27.6 percent of Hispanics live in extended families, compared to 22.4 percent of African Americans and 14.9 percent of whites.

A *blended family* consists of one or more children living with a biological or adoptive parent and an unrelated stepparent who are married to one another. In the US, 8.7 percent of families are considered blended with little variance across racial groups.

A *cohabiting family* consists of one or more children living with a biological or adoptive parent and an unrelated adult who lives with the parent. About 3 percent of families in the US are in this category (although this type of family structure is growing rapidly).

A *single adult/parent family* consists of one or more children living with a single adult (male or female, related or unrelated to the child or children). In the United States, 16.3 percent of all families are led by a single parent, including 37.5 percent of African American children, 15.3 percent of Hispanic children, and 11.2 percent of white children.

An *unmarried biological or adoptive family* consists of one or more children living with two parents who are not married to one another and are both biological or adoptive parents to all children in the family. Only about 1–2 percent of all racial groups in the US fit into this category.

The *other family* consists of one or more children living with related or unrelated adults who are not biological or adoptive parents. Children raised by their grandparents are included in this category, as are foster children. About 3 percent of all families in the US are so designated, including 6.3 percent of African Americans, 3.8 percent of Hispanics, and 2.1 percent of whites.

One category not included in the NCHS survey is a *polygamous family*, which typically consists of a husband who is married to multiple wives (and some with concubines who are not married to the husband). In certain communities in the Middle East and Africa, a significant percentage of the population may live in this type of family structure. It is illegal in many countries but is still practiced underground.

Case Studies of the Various Family Structures

The statistics I've used thus far from many sources to illustrate how families have been changing don't tell the whole story. To truly understand what's happening in families today, one must examine them from the inside to see how their family structures affect their lives. In the United States, the picture today is one of turbulence. Andrew Cherlin, in his book *The Marriage-Go-Round*, points out that Americans are more likely to marry and then divorce than any other group in the world. He attributes this phenomenon to two incompatible beliefs Americans hold:

  » Having a companion or soul mate is important for happiness.
  » Being in a spousal or significant-other relationship that doesn't meet personal needs or restricts freedom warrants going elsewhere to have those needs met.[2]

Americans are therefore simultaneously too eager to marry and too willing to divorce or end a significant relationship. He sees this instability in marriage (as well as cohabitation) as particularly problematic for today's children when he writes, "Although marriage is important, slowing down the process of partnering would, I am convinced, be in the best interests of American children. We should make stable families a policy priority regardless of how many parents are present in the home."[3] For Cherlin, the continual movement of adults in and out of children's lives as they enter into new relationships deleteriously affects the children's emotional well-being. Other studies by Annette Lareau and more recently Robert Putnam have highlighted the challenges single mothers and cohabiters have in raising children.[4] In Lareau's book titled *Unequal Childhoods: Class, Race, and Family Life* she describes the different child rearing practices as well as the significant advantages children from two-parent homes have as compared to children in single-mother or cohabiting homes. According to her study, in stable family structures headed by two parents, children did better in school and were better adjusted to societal demands. Putnam saw similar dynamics as he compared families with different structures from across the United States. Putnam argues that strong, stable family structures lead to increased opportunities and higher well-being for children, while children in unstable family environments—typically homes led by single mothers or headed by cohabiters—often have difficulty meeting their day-to-day needs and struggle to become successful adults, all of which leads to income inequality.

My research team and I also wanted to explore the impact of family structure on family functioning and, in particular, to answer the question: How do the various family structures affect a family's human, social, and financial capital? We decided to conduct several case studies with individuals who had experienced different family structures and explore with them how their family structure affected their family capital. These case studies are not based on a random sample nor do they represent all families with a certain structure. They come from a "convenience sample"—families my research team were aware of that existed in a particular structure. Initially we thought that it would be fairly easy to identify people living in different family structures, take their case histories, and then describe the basic dynamics of the particular family types. However, as we began to interview these people and take their case histories it became clear that all but one of them had lived in several different family structures over their lifetimes. Much like Cherlin noted in his book, we saw that movement between different family structures was much more common than living in one structure for a long period. Thus, each of the five case studies—with the exception of the first case study of a nuclear family—describes movement between family structures, and the case studies are titled based on the different family structures the person has experienced. All the case studies are disguised to protect the anonymity of the interviewees.

As you read each case study, ask yourself the following questions:

» How does the family structure enhance or undermine family capital? Does it strengthen children and provide the family with more resources?

» How did a change in family structure affect the individuals involved? For example, did moving from a nuclear family to a blended family or single-mother family enhance or undermine family capital? If so, in what ways?

You'll note that some individuals chose to change their family structure whereas others had the change thrust upon them, through actions outside their control. After each case study, I will briefly comment on the pertinent family capital.

Traditional Nuclear Family: The Case of Joan and Adam

Joan grew up in northern Arizona with six siblings. Her dad was an accountant in a large accounting firm and her mother was a homemaker who involved herself in community theater. Joan's family valued the arts and learning. She spent most of her youth dancing, singing and acting in shows, and participating in many dance competitions. She and her sisters especially excelled in ballet. Joan's mother drove the girls to all their lessons, and her dad started a construction business to provide a second income for the family. Joan's grandmother also helped pay for ballet lessons when money was tight. Joan became a dance major in college. During the next few years, she performed dance routines in a number of college events and became well known in the university community for her skill in dancing.

In 1994, Joan was asked to teach ballet classes at a local studio. Over the next few years, she expanded the dance curriculum at a local college, became a certified dance teacher, graduated from college, married, and created a business called the School of Ballet.

Adam, Joan's husband, grew up in a suburban neighborhood in Michigan with four siblings. His father was a professor at the local college and his mother taught elementary school for a year after graduating from college before transitioning to full-time homemaker and mother. They both expected their children to work hard and do well in school. Adam actively participated in the Boy Scouts of America and achieved the rank of Eagle Scout. He also enjoyed playing on computers. He graduated near the top of his high school class and earned a scholarship to college. It certainly helped that both his parents could help him with his schoolwork. Adam spent time in South America serving in the Peace Corps, met and married Joan, and eventually completed his undergraduate and master's degree in business administration. Three of Adam's four siblings have college degrees and two have master's degrees.

When Adam graduated with his master's degree, he and Joan had two children and Joan was teaching about fifty dance students at a local studio. Joan took care of all the teaching and interfacing with the students, while Adam took care of the business and technical side. Because few certified dance teachers were in their area, and because the demand for dance instruction seemed to be growing, Joan and Adam decided they would build a dance business locally rather than pursuing Adam's job possibilities out of state. Both Joan's and Adam's families were supportive of their decision to start a dance business.

Joan and Adam wanted to purchase a home with enough space for a studio so Joan could teach without sacrificing too much family time,

but with student loans and no job, purchasing a home would be difficult—if not impossible—on their own. Joan's father, who was involved
in real estate in Arizona, helped locate, negotiate, and finance a house
that had a 1,600-foot woodshop behind it. To turn the woodshop into
a studio, permits had to be obtained from the city, utilities had to be
brought up from the house, retaining walls needed to be built, and the
inside needed a complete makeover to bring it up to code.

Adam's family held a family reunion to help convert the woodshop
into a studio; his siblings built a retaining wall and did the outside
work, and Adam's brother-in-law ran the heavy equipment. Joan's
family then had a family reunion with her parents and siblings also
helping with the studio. One of her siblings is a professional contractor, so they were able to do the utilities and large structural work.
Adam, Joan, and her father finished the painting, flooring, and final
details over the summer. Seven months after the house was purchased,
the studio was ready for classes.

The next three years were stressful and challenging for Joan and
Adam. The cost of the studio remodel took nearly all the money they
had in reserve. The time Adam put into the business had cost him
opportunities in the job market and being tied down by the dance studio severely limited his career options and income. Eventually, Joan
and Adam had two more children, which they strategically planned
to fit into Joan's busy schedule. But even with careful planning Joan
couldn't take more than a few weeks off from classes. The business was
slowly growing, but Adam was unemployed for eighteen of the first
thirty-six months the studio was in operation. Paying for the mort-
gage, utilities, and food made finances extremely tight. Adam's father
provided emotional support throughout Adam's employment frustration and he eventually found a solid job for him that matched his skill
set. The lean and uncertain years pushed Adam and Joan to be very
frugal in their shopping habits. They purchased used cars with cash
only and were able to pay off their house in ten years.

Their business has since grown to over two hundred students
who compete in regional, national, and world competitions. The

business has continued to require significant investments: $30,000 for landscaping, $17,000 to pave the road, $5,000 for new flooring, and travel expenses to attend competitions. Joan and Adam's family still revolves around the business. Adam has to have flexible work so he can shovel the snow in the winter, fix things in the studio, and manage the technical side of the business. Vacations are planned around dance competitions or during the one month in the summer when classes aren't in session. Joan occasionally leaves for weekends to judge competitions, which somewhat complicates the family schedule.

Adam and Joan have taken on different roles over the years. Joan was home with the kids when they were young, and Adam's mother came to the house once or twice a week to care for the kids when Joan was teaching. Since the kids have gotten older, Joan doesn't see them for very long in the afternoon before she has to go to class. Adam picks up the older kids from school and takes them to their various activities. He is responsible for evening meals on weekdays since Joan is teaching during those hours and often can't eat with the family. From the time the kids turned eight, they were expected to cook a dinner meal and clean it up once a week. Joan and Adam have had to limit the extracurricular activities of their children because of the constraints of their business. Joan volunteers during the day at the kids' school and Adam is mainly responsible to help the kids with homework.

Parenting is extremely important to Adam and Joan, and they have both read many books on the topic. They try to be available whenever necessary, while giving the kids space to play on their own. The children are expected to work hard in everything they do. When the kids ask, "why do we have to do this?" the response is always, "you don't *have* to do this, you *get* to do it." Adam and Joan try to resist any sort of perfectionist mindset and instead teach their children that mistakes are expected and acceptable as long as they understand and correct them. Adam often says, "that is what failure looks like," when he or anyone else makes a mistake. The kids are expected to take responsibility for their mistakes, like when the oldest daughter kicked a soccer ball through a window and had to help buy the materials and repair it.

Continuous learning is extremely important to the family, including formal education. The children all attended a K–8 charter school with a program for stringed musical instruments and very strong math and science programs. The children are expected to manage themselves and get all their homework done, though their parents are always willing to help. The older children attend an accelerated high school where they will graduate from high school with an associate degree and are expected to complete a bachelor's degree. Adam and Joan will pay for each child's college tuition as long as they are putting in the necessary effort to get good grades and pursue a worthwhile career.

The family values working hard and playing hard together. During the summers, the entire family wakes up at 7:00 a.m., exercises for an hour, and works in the yard for thirty minutes before eating breakfast. Adam and Joan do physically and mentally challenging outdoor activities with the family, such as skiing, mountain biking, camping, hiking, and scuba diving. The two older children have had the opportunity to travel to Europe with their grandparents, but they were required to pay for their airline tickets and had to learn German beforehand. At home, the children help renovate the house, fix the studio as needed, and shovel snow off the seventy-five-foot driveway in the winter.

Adam and Joan don't pay their children for housework or give them an allowance, although they do pay for clothes and education-related expenses. The children earn money by helping teach dance classes, helping with the business, or doing activities the parents think will help them learn and grow, such as taking free online college-level classes, learning German, reading business books, learning programs such as Adobe Photoshop, and building apps with Adam. Adam constantly negotiates with the children when they want something so that they understand how the real world works.

Commentary

The role of family capital is fairly clear in the case of Joan and Adam. Without the support of her parents and the financial support of her grandmother, Joan wouldn't have been able to develop her dance talents that allowed her to start her own dance studio. The help from Joan's father to finance their new home with the dance studio and the labor of the large, extended family to make the studio a reality likewise exemplify family capital. Moreover, Joan and Adam have prioritized developing their children's talents and giving them experiences to become successful adults. In this stable family situation, Adam and Joan have developed significant human, social, and financial capital within their family. Much of this is due to a parenting style that focuses on mentoring the children, requiring them to demonstrate responsibility, and giving them opportunities to develop themselves.

Traditional to Single-Parent to Blended Family: The Case of Svetlana

In 1997, while in their early twenties, Svetlana and George Zubo left their Polish homeland with their two-year-old son, George Jr., to find work in the United States. Fortunately, George obtained a US work visa and thus the Zubo family came to America legally. After arriving in the US, George found a good job in the construction industry and the Zubos were able to buy a small home where they eventually welcomed four additional children—all girls—by 2005. Things were going well by all accounts until early in 2006 when George left Svetlana for a new girlfriend and filed for divorce. Svetlana was devastated and initially fought the divorce, but eventually signed the divorce papers in exchange for George's $750 monthly child support payment.

Once the divorce was final and George moved out, Svetlana had to start a new life on her own and provide for her five children. Unfortunately, she had few marketable skills with which to supplement child support. But she found work cleaning homes for wealthy homeowners (mostly in the early mornings) and ran a daycare center out of her home. Between the child support and her own income generating activities, the family income was about $2,500 per month—not a lot of money to meet the needs of a family of six, especially since the mortgage and utilities for Svetlana's home were $1,300 per month.

Fortunately for Svetlana, George continued to be fairly active in the children's lives—he took them every other weekend, bought them birthday presents, attended their school activities, and was available when they needed advice. To supplement the family's income, Svetlana's son, George, provided the family with $200 a month by working a part-time job while in high school. Svetlana was also able to draw upon the government for medical insurance (Medicaid) for her children. However, she indicated that for some years she didn't report all her income on tax returns in order to keep her children on the insurance. (Children can lose their Medicaid benefits if the family makes too much money.) Svetlana also had met regularly with the local Catholic bishop; he provided her with spiritual guidance and emotional support. She took her children to Catholic mass and got them involved in church-sponsored activities. In some instances, when Svetlana faced significant financial difficulties, the Catholic bishop arranged for financial assistance, and, on one occasion, volunteers from the local parish repaired plumbing in her home. Svetlana also had a number of friends who helped her emotionally and, at times, financially during her transition to being a single mother. Even though the financial resources dwindled significantly due to the divorce, she was able to garner resources from her son, the government, the local church, and her friends. Thus she weathered financial storms much better than many single mothers. Largely due to that, Svetlana's children did fairly well in school. Moreover, the continued support from her ex-husband mitigated, to a degree, the emotional wounds that often afflict children when parents divorce.

After ten years of being single and having several boyfriends (who were somewhat disruptive to Svetlana and her children), Svetlana remarried in 2016. She met Victor at a local church-sponsored picnic and they hit it off. Victor has a good job as an auto mechanic making about $45,000 per year and his income, along with the child support payments, has allowed Svetlana to return to being a stay-at-home mom (which is her preference). Another important benefit of this new union for Svetlana is that Victor is a US citizen; her immigration status had been unclear since her divorce from George. Svetlana's marriage thus made it less likely she would be deported, and she could eventually achieve citizenship. Victor has one son from a previous marriage, age twenty-seven, who lives in another state, so while Svetlana's new family is technically blended, her children haven't had to adjust to living with new siblings. Victor says that taking on the responsibility as the father to five children has been a challenge, but he also notes his relationships with Svetlana and with the children, while not perfect, are on solid footing. He also keeps track of his biological son and gives him some support—both financial and emotional—when needed. His son attended his wedding with Svetlana and seems supportive of his stepmother and stepsiblings.

Commentary

Fortunately, after her divorce Svetlana was able to draw upon resources from the government, the Catholic Church, and her friends, which substituted for the family capital she lacked. In the end, a new marriage with a stable partner has created a much more secure environment for Svetlana and her children. They seem to be thriving as a new blended family. Moreover, the size of the family increased by adding members from Victor's family—potentially leading to more resources.

Traditional Marriage to Extended Family to Same-Sex Cohabiting Relationship: The Case of John

John grew up in a rural farming community, where his father competed in professional rodeo competitions and owned an excavation business and his mother was employed as a bank clerk. They didn't have a lot of money, but John's mother managed their funds wisely and John didn't feel like they were poor. Both sets of grandparents, who lived in the same town, heavily influenced his life. They were devout, very hardworking, and devoted to their marriages. From quite a young age, John decided he wanted to be successful like his grandparents were.

John's mother, very active and available as a parent, pushed her three children to succeed. She was passionate about education and expected John and his two siblings to graduate from college. John spent a lot of his time in the outdoors with his family. At the age of eleven he was waking up at 5:00 a.m. to work on the farm, and by the time he was seventeen he was working sixteen-hour days. However, at age fifteen John's life changed dramatically when his parents divorced.

John's mother quickly remarried a man who had five children. Together they had two more children, making a total of ten. John lived with his mother and stepfather until he went to college. During that time, the entire family involved themselves in their local church. John's stepfather had strong entrepreneurial skills, helping small businesses grow. His mother continued to push education, and all of John's biological siblings graduated from college. The arts were very important in his family; John went to college on a voice scholarship. He also excelled as a writer and was on the debate team, where he met Susan, the girl he would later marry.

John attended a private university in a neighboring state on schol-arship. Three years into his college education, John's biological father passed away. The death traumatized John, and he dropped out of col-lege, working part-time for a year before returning to the university. He intended to go to law school, but in an odd twist of fate his path changed dramatically. One of John's roommates (Brandon, an entre-preneurial fifty-five-year-old man) headed the aviation program at a local college. One day Brandon took John flying in a small airplane and John was hooked. Brandon asked John to work for him by creat-ing and writing an aviation course to train pilots. John dropped out of school for the job, which he held while working toward his pilot's license. The curriculum was a great success for the college and for John. He received royalties of 20 percent.

While working with Brandon and on his own as a pilot, John reconnected with Susan; that's when they decided to get married. Her family was also entrepreneurial and devoutly religious. Susan, who had finished law school and worked as an attorney, had three children with John over the next few years. Both John and Susan immersed themselves in parenthood.

In 1997, Brandon and John decided to grow the business by selling it online to other universities. Susan supported John in his venture and pushed him to work on the business. Because of John's strong work ethic and exceptional writing ability, he was able to write about twenty pages a day. The business was a huge success, with the program winning multiple national awards for the college. John soon made $500,000 per year, and he bought an 8,000-square-foot home that became the hub for the family. John's stepfather and mother had some financial difficulties, so John welcomed them and their two youngest children into his home. His parents ended up staying for five years. During that time John and Susan were both working, so John's mother took care of their kids. They had family dinners every night and enjoyed long discussions together. John eventually hired his stepfather, which caused some friction because Susan and John's stepfather didn't always agree on how the business should be run.

In early 2008, John disclosed to his wife that he had come to question his sexual orientation and thought he was gay. He told her that he loved her despite his feelings, had always been completely faithful, and had never acted on his those feelings. Susan reacted with grief and concern, but they decided to stay together and figure out how to deal with the situation, for the sake of their children. John wasn't planning to tell anyone else, but the information quickly spread among family, friends, and the community. Their parents wanted them to stay together, but other family members thought they should separate.

Five months after he came out to Susan, the stress, grief, and pressure from family and community members had grown so strong that John moved out of the house. They soon divorced and were granted joint custody of the children. John remained very involved in his children's lives, but when Susan remarried a few years later he allowed her to take the children to a neighboring state, believing that doing so would provide a stable life for the children. He is still actively involved in their parenting and sees them frequently.

Although his familial relationships and support remained strong, John felt like he was ostracized by some of his former friends and associates. He eventually lost most of his friends in the community and in his religious group. John has rejected the "broken person" and victim narratives people projected onto him. A very successful gay uncle of John had been with his partner for over twenty years, so John talked with him.

Shortly after moving out of his house, John moved in with Edward, his partner. Edward's parents had divorced when he was seven; his mother is now in her eighth marriage, while his father is in his fifth. Edward had grown up in a religious atmosphere, but he became antagonistic toward religion after coming out. John has developed some spiritual practices on his own, but he doesn't belong to any organized religion. John and Edward have been together for about eight years now. John says the biggest problems they face in their relationship come mostly from their different backgrounds.

In 2010, the college canceled John's business contract. Susan and John's stepfather worked with John to try to get accreditation so that he could sell the program himself. The process of accreditation was costing him about $100,000 a month, so he liquidated all his assets to fund the business while he waited to get federal funding. In 2012, however, the federal funding he hoped for was discontinued, and even though John had completed 90 percent of the requirements for accreditation, he ran out of money and had to declare bankruptcy. He said, "I lost everything but my relationships."

After losing the business he had spent more than twenty years building, John fell into a deep depression. A friend he met in an online chatroom for gay fathers helped him through his emotional turmoil. John took seasonal work at a local resort and then other low-level work, before finishing his college degree and returning to piloting. John has again worked his way up to a six-figure salary. John and Edward haven't married due to financial reasons associated with the bankruptcy, and John isn't sure if they ever will. John remains deeply devoted as a parent and makes sure his kids are well cared for. Edward doesn't try to parent the children when they are with John. Sometimes people ask the children how Edward is related to them; they just say they aren't really sure.

John still fondly remembers the time with his original family and his parents in his large home. His entrepreneurial spirit is still strong and he said he "always has stuff brewing." Since he came out, he has much less access to people and finances in the community: "I used to be able to call up so many successful friends, but now they won't even take my calls." Even so, John approaches everything with a strong work ethic and determination, so he is confident the future will be bright.

Commentary

John has maintained some semblance of stability and preserved some family capital despite his divorce and transition to a cohabiting, gay relationship, as evidenced by the continued help John received from his ex-wife and stepfather with the business—even though those efforts eventually failed. His relationship with Edward is stable, having lasted eight years, but they have no plans to marry. Little evidence suggests Edward's family has provided this new relationship with any significant resources, but they appear emotionally supportive. Through his extended family, John's gay uncle has helped him transition to being openly gay. However, as is sometimes the case when a relationship goes against a community's norms, John's diminished access to his former friends hurts his capital in the community. The relationship he's maintained with his children has enhanced his family capital, however, and has also helped to create more stability in his life.

Cohabitating Relationship to Single Mom to Extended Family: The Case of Maria

Maria's mother was a victim of domestic violence. Eventually, her mother, Rosa, divorced her father after suffering a broken nose during one of his attacks. Thus, when Maria was age seven, Rosa raised her and her older sister, Luz (age nine), alone. Two years after the divorce her mother met Fredo, an accountant with a steady job, and Rosa and the two girls moved in with him in a cohabiting relationship. Fredo supported Maria and Luz and provided them with some stability. More

importantly, he was a kind and gentle partner to Rosa, and they eventually married after living together for five years.

As Maria moved into her teenage years she began to rebel, starting with cigarettes and alcohol and then moving on to marijuana and
other recreational drugs. Her sister Luz was a heroin addict at age eighteen and spent much of her time in various rehab facilities. After high
school, Maria moved out on her own and worked at several minimum
wage retail jobs. She had several boyfriends and usually moved in with
them, which helped her financially. Unfortunately, as had been the
case with her mother's first marriage, her boyfriends were invariably
abusive—both emotionally and physically. Once the abuse started,
Maria was aware enough to leave those relationships but not without
many emotional scars. In particular, she had difficulty trusting and
forming long-term, supportive relationships with men.

At age twenty-four, Maria met Tony, who seemed to be her ideal
partner: he was going to school to get a degree, held a good part-time
job, and treated her well. After dating for a few months, Maria moved
in with Tony. Five months later she got pregnant, which changed their
relationship. Because Tony didn't know how he would provide for a
child, he felt trapped. Tensions about the pregnancy led to their sepa-
ration, and Maria moved back to live with Rosa and Fredo to prepare
to have her baby.

Maria had the baby, Anita, in 2016; the little girl was diagnosed
with severe autism that will require constant care. Maria doesn't
know whether she will eventually be able to work to provide for herself and her daughter. Tony has not seen the baby, apparently wants
no contact, and is reluctant to pay child support (with little money
to give). Fortunately for Maria, both Rosa and Fredo have told her
that she can live with them and that they will help raise Anita. Maria,
although grateful for such help, nevertheless has an uncertain future
ahead: a woman with a special-needs child may find attracting a marriage partner difficult, and the living arrangement with her mother
and stepfather has an uncertain duration. But at this point, given her
financial situation, she has no other options.

Commentary

Maria's story is common for young women today who have children out of wedlock; the boyfriend decides to move on, leaving the mother with the responsibility to care for the child. Bereft of resources, Maria had to ask her mother and stepfather to take her in and help raise the baby. Like Maria, many single mothers today live with parents or grandparents who are literally life-savers—providing them with food, shelter, childcare assistance, and emotional support. Unfortunately, despite the family capital Maria has available to her, her prospects for becoming independent and creating her own family capital are not good (given her lack of skills and Anita's special needs). Thus, Maria is likely to be living with Rosa and Fredo for many years to come.

Traditional Marriage to a Variety of Family Structures: The Case of Robert

Robert was raised in the suburbs of a big city in a stable home with his parents and five siblings. His father was a college-educated engineer who could fix anything, and his mother was an excellent cook who kept the house in order. Even though Robert's parents came from different religious backgrounds, they attended the same worship services and were very involved in the religious community. His parents supported Robert whenever he wanted to try something new. His father taught him to fix cars, and he learned a lot of construction skills when they built an addition on their home.

Robert works hard and likes solving problems. He trusts his family and friends. When he thinks he's right about something, Robert forcefully makes his point and won't let the issue go. Robert didn't enjoy being under the thumb of authority so he disliked school; due to his intelligence and work ethic, however, he easily graduated from high school. He went to college for a year before deciding it wasn't for him.

Amelia, Robert's future wife, was the older of two children. Her father, a doctor, passed away when she was young. He had a substantial life insurance policy so the family had enough money to continue living in a wealthy community. Her mother, a socialite with many social engagements, hired a nanny to raise Amelia and her younger sibling. Unfortunately, Amelia got involved with drugs, sex, and alcohol while in high school. She wasn't much of a student, and most of her skills were in the social arena. After graduating from high school she had no desire to go on to college.

When Robert and Amelia met, he was twenty-three and she was nineteen. Robert had moved back to his parents' home, working part-time while figuring out what to do with his life. Amelia was living in her car and doing drugs while dating various men. Robert started dating Amelia and she ended up moving in with his family. Because Amelia grew up with a nanny who did all the housework, she never learned any domestic skills. Soon Amelia's lack of cleanliness, habit of borrowing things without asking, ability to get Robert to do whatever she wanted, and late night make-out sessions on the couch with him began to irritate Robert's family.

Six months after Amelia moved in, Robert and Amelia married and moved to a small apartment. Robert's dad, troubled because Robert didn't have a career plan, helped him get his contractor's license. Robert and Amelia had three children in quick succession. Robert was deeply motivated to provide for his family and worked extremely hard. Amelia was overwhelmed by her new responsibilities. The house was constantly a mess, with dirty diapers left wherever they were changed. Meals weren't prepared regularly, and the kids weren't cared for very well. She wasn't used to financial constraints, so she spent their money as fast as Robert made it.

Robert did well with remodeling work, but he really started making money after his dad helped him purchase a house to fix up and resell. Robert remodeled and upgraded the house and sold it two years later. Because the real estate market was so hot in that area, and because of the tax code, he ended up making over $100,000 from the sale. Robert's drive, business skills, and risk-taking ability were perfect for the market. He hired four people for his crew and within a short time he was making over $100,000 a year from remodeling. Robert then changed his focus from construction to utility work and made some investments in that area.

Robert felt he was contributing much more to the family than Amelia was, which created a lot of friction. When he came home from work he usually found the babies in dirty diapers, the house a disaster, and everyone hungry. Almost every night he'd either make or buy dinner and then put the kids to bed. Robert's family and Amelia's friends would sometimes come over and clean the house in hopes that Amelia would try to keep it that way, but she never seemed interested. Robert's frustration led him to ask his family and friends for advice, but nothing changed.

Robert enjoyed camping, boating, and motorsports with his children. They spent a great deal of time with Robert's family, and Robert relied on his family for help with the kids. Since Robert hadn't liked school, he didn't push his children toward education. Amelia enjoyed the fun family activities, but she withdrew when things were unpleasant or hard. She tried to live the social life she had seen her mother live, so the children were often left to fend for themselves. Robert finally recognized that Amelia was unreliable so he stopped counting on her for anything.

Robert saw an opportunity to expand his utility business in a neighboring state. He was confident it would be a great financial opportunity and also thought it might help their marriage if they moved farther from their families. A month before the move, Robert discovered Amelia was sleeping with one of the men on his crew. He aborted the move and took his three children to live with his parents; Amelia stayed in the house a few miles away. Robert fired his crew member and drastically reduced his workload so he could care for his children. In the process, he lost an opportunity that would have probably yielded hundreds of thousands of dollars. His parents helped as much as they could with meals, cleaning, and childcare, but they still had a child at home who needed their time and attention.

Robert really wanted to keep his family together, so he lived with his parents for a year while he and Amelia worked on their relationship. They reconciled but continued to struggle in many areas. Robert hired a maid so Amelia could contribute in ways besides housekeeping. They bought an apartment building as an investment, with Amelia agreeing to manage it. With some financing from Robert's dad, they also purchased a small house, which they planned to tear down and replace with a larger house that they could sell. Robert and Amelia moved into Robert's parents' home while they built the investment house, thus helping to alleviate their financial, housework, and trust issues.

While living with Robert's parents, Amelia had their fourth child. Robert's parents talked to Robert and Amelia about their expectations of cleanliness, but nothing changed. Amelia didn't seem to comprehend the need to help with housework, so Robert's parents ended up bearing the increased burden.

A year later, Robert and Amelia moved into the beautiful new home he had built. Things were looking up, but it was 2008—the real estate market soon took a dive. Robert's construction work evaporated almost completely. He liquidated some of his real estate investments to avoid losing them. Amelia hadn't managed the apartment building well, so they lost the entire $200,000 investment. Although Robert's income had plunged, Amelia wasn't prepared to curb her spending habits, nor had her housekeeping abilities improved. The huge house quickly became a huge mess.

As a sailing enthusiast, Robert saw an opportunity to make money buying, fixing, and reselling boats. The money wasn't as good as it had been in construction, but it was all in cash and allowed him to pay the necessary bills each month. During these hard times, Amelia became more and more reclusive, spending her time in her room, on social media, or doing drugs. As the economy picked up, Robert returned to construction and made good money. After having lived in their house for four years, they finally sold it and made almost $1,000,000 in profit. Shortly after selling the house, Robert learned that Amelia had been using social media to hook up with different men. After talking with his older children, he decided to divorce Amelia.

Robert tried to make the divorce as amicable as possible to protect his children. Amelia was awarded over $500,000 from the sale of the house, $4,000 a month in alimony and child support, and shared custody of the kids. Robert's family gave him whatever support they could. After the divorce his dad helped him buy properties to fix up and he was soon back to making good money.

Working out the logistical details concerning the children and caring for them whenever they were with him challenged Robert. Amelia continued to be very relaxed in her parenting. The children would often skip school because she didn't wake them up and put them on the bus. Robert made sure his children went to school at least when they were at his house. Robert's family helped care for the children and had them over for meals and activities often. Amelia adjusted poorly to not being part of the family and complained to her children about not being invited to family events. The divorce hurt his relationship with his children, especially with his oldest daughter.

Robert wasn't actively looking to remarry, but that didn't stop people from trying to set him up. After two years of single life, he started dating a widow, Helen, with four children. They got married, but right after the wedding, Helen made it clear that she didn't want to deal with Robert's children. He tried to work things out with her but three months after the wedding, the marriage was over. Robert's family had been very excited about the marriage, and they were disappointed when it failed.

A year after his second divorce, Robert started dating Gloria, a divorced woman with two young children. Gloria had moved in with her parents following her divorce and had gone back to college for a master's degree. Her parents provided financial support as well as childcare. Gloria didn't belong to the same religious community as Robert, which concerned some of his family members. Gloria's children would throw tantrums and hit other kids to get what they wanted, which caused friction during family gatherings with Robert's family. As Gloria and Robert continued dating, Robert began to discipline her children. The different parenting styles the children experienced complicated the situation.

After a year of dating, Robert and Gloria got engaged and moved in together, much to the chagrin of some in his family. After six months, they got married. At the wedding, Robert's family and friends expressed their hopes that this marriage would succeed, since "Robert deserves some happiness after all his hard work." Robert says he is 100 percent committed to this new marriage and is very optimistic that he will finally have a supportive wife. Robert is rebounding quite well financially, but the divorces have taken a toll on him, both financially and emotionally.

Commentary

Robert's family structure has been turbulent: he has been in three traditional marriages, become a single parent, been a part of extended and blended families, and been in a cohabiting relationship. However, his parents have been highly supportive of him, his wives, and his children. They have tended the children, provided Robert with investment funds, let his family live with them, and provided significant social and emotional support for Robert and his children. In terms of family capital, the divorces have put a significant drain on Robert's finances (although such funds certainly have helped his ex-wives and children). In this case, the role of the parents in providing support for Robert and his family has probably been the most important aspect of family capital.

Family Structure and Its Impact on Family Stability and the Family Network

Research on family structures, along with information from our case studies, allows us to plot various family structures, which are found in figure 3.1 (opposite).

The Family Network

On the horizontal axis polygamous, extended, and blended families are at the "larger" end of the scale, since they tend to create large family networks. As was the case with Svetlana and Robert in their blended families, these family structures have the potential of linking members from multiple families together in a large social network. Robert and

Figure 3.1 Family Structures, Family Stability, and Family Network Size

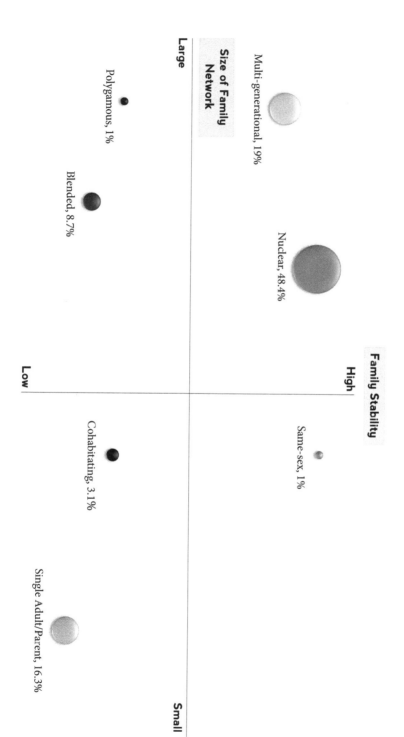

Maria's family size also increased when they lived with their parents, creating multi-generational, extended family units. While not always the case, these three family structures could generate family capital due to large familial networks. Traditional families like Joan and Adam's vary greatly in terms of family size so they are plotted closer to the middle of the horizontal axis.

In contrast, same-sex married couples, cohabiting partners, and single parents will likely have smaller family networks. Same-sex couples often rely on surrogates, artificial insemination, or adoption as a way of adding children. Research on cohabitation indicates that cohabiting couples have less contact with parents than do couples in traditional marriages.[5] Since much of a family's social network flows through the parents, the lack of contact with parents can limit family networks.

Finally, the single-parent structure is disadvantaged in terms of family networks. While there are exceptions in which the noncustodial parent's family is highly involved with a single parent—generally the mother—more often, as in the case of the father of Maria's baby, the noncustodial parent and family have no contact and provide no support—financial or otherwise. When half of a family network is eliminated, creating a large network of family support is difficult.

Family Stability

Family stability is determined by how long a couple stays together in a harmonious relationship that provides continued support for children and other family members. Unfortunately, as the case studies indicate, family stability is in short supply, as also discussed in chapter 2. Marriage is the most stable form of union. Same-sex married couples in Europe, where a longer history of same-sex marriages exists than in the United States, experience about the same divorce rate as traditional couples do.[6]

Historically, extended families were fairly stable as children lived with their parents. Eventually the children matured, married, continued to live with their parents, and then took care of their parents as they grew older and needed more help. I saw this pattern as typical in Japan in the early 1970s. Multi-generational, extended families are still common today, but the more likely scenario is found in Robert's case study where he, his wife, and his children lived with his parents for several months while in transition or experiencing a crisis. In my own family, two daughters, their husbands, and their four children lived with me recently for several months as the husbands were making work and schooling transitions. Other children and their spouses as well as a sister-in-law have lived with us over the years. In 2008, my wife's parents lived with us for a year because my father-in-law was in poor health.

Studies show that second marriages are less stable than first marriages (60 percent end in divorce), and third marriages are even less so (73 percent end in divorce).[7] With some exceptions, people don't get better at marriage the more they marry.[8] Thus, blended families appear on the grid in a less stable position than those in first marriage relationships or those in multi-generational families. In Robert's case, his divorce from Helen was precipitated by her unwillingness to play the role of mother to his children in their blended family.

Chapter 2 described the research on cohabiting couples, noting that these relationships are highly unstable. Three of our case studies—Maria, Robert, and John—exemplify this movement in and out of cohabiting relationships. John, however, is an exception since his cohabiting relationship with Edward has lasted more than eight years. Svetlana's case highlights the instability of being a single parent. When cohabiting, new boyfriends or girlfriends may enter the picture, which creates uncertainty for the children. In many cases, there are multiple boyfriends or girlfriends simultaneously, which leads to further uncertainty and instability.

Can You Create Stability and a Network if Your Family Structure Lacks Family Capital?

Some of you who are not fortunate enough to be in an advantageous family structure may ask, "Am I doomed to failure in creating family capital?" Absolutely not! One of the best examples of someone who faced significant odds in developing family capital was my grandmother, Wyroa Hansen. Wyroa, left with four small children and few resources after her husband Clarence died from appendicitis, wanted to create a stable and supportive environment for her children. So she enlisted the help of her mother (also a widow) and her siblings—particularly her oldest brother, Reese—to provide childcare and emotional support for her children. My mother, Bonnie, often spoke about Reese as a surrogate father to her and her siblings. Wyroa's mother, Helena, also helped her obtain a teaching certificate by watching Wyroa's children during several summers when Wyroa moved to the city for the summer to further her education. With the large, extended Hansen family also supporting Wyroa and her children, they provided for Wyroa's family financially, socially, and emotionally.

Wyroa decided not to marry until all of her children had left her home. Nevertheless, Wyroa met Robert Done and dated him for ten years, which avoided some of the challenges and disruption that can come with a blended family. He supported Wyroa and her children during that time. Bob brought his youngest son into the marriage, but the stepsiblings never lived in the same home with each other since Wyroa's three daughters were married adults.

Wyroa is a good example of a single mother who developed a family network and created stable family relationships, even though her situation was not conducive to creating family capital. However, if Wyroa had believed she and Bob could have succeeded in putting a blended family together, she and her children might have had more financial, social, and emotional support—and less hardship associated with single parenthood—if she had not delayed marriage.

How Can I Create a Successful Family Structure?

If you are single, the key decision is whether to marry (or be in a committed relationship) or to remain single. Of course, you cannot know for sure if a good fit for a life-long partner will come into your life. Nevertheless, I typically encourage those I counsel to at least explore the possibility of a committed partnership and actively socialize and date potential mates. I find that many young people these days spend too much time on their cell phones and with social media, making connecting with a real-live human being and developing a lasting relationship difficult. Exploring new relationships can leave you emotionally vulnerable, but I believe it is worth the risk. Having a partner to share life's challenges with brings great satisfaction and joy.

Regardless of what decision you make regarding your relationships, expanding and developing your family network is important. Thus, I encourage people who want to develop their family capital to put together a pedigree chart, preferably for three generations, to identify who is actually in the family network. Firms such as Ancestry.com, with their software, simplify the process of charting genealogy and tracking down relatives. The next step is to identify the type of relationship you have with those in the chart, from very close to nonexistent. Then come up with a plan to develop relationships with family members you want to get closer to, whether through personal visits, emails, Facebook, or some other medium. You might feel somewhat awkward at first reaching out to someone you don't know, but I'm surprised at how many people are delighted when they learn of a family connection to someone new. The connection to a family member, even if it's distant, can prove quite powerful. Even if you decide not to marry or find a long-term partner, actively managing your family network and relationships can enhance family capital.

You also need to consider whether to have children. Offspring require work and are very costly, so the issue should not be taken lightly. Theresa and I faced stiff challenges raising seven children—the time, worries, and money. However, the satisfaction in seeing my children grow, develop, and succeed (as well as fail) has provided me with insights and experiences that I would never have had otherwise. And as I'm in the middle of my seventh decade on this planet, my children are now providing Theresa and me with the kind of emotional and social support that we provided them when they were children. For some couples, adoption offers another route to children. My brother Jeff and my daughter Emily have found adoption to be very satisfying, as well as challenging. The process for qualifying for and finding a potential adoptee is difficult and can put you on an emotional roller-coaster of uncertainty. Having children is an intensely personal matter, so I encourage couples to understand the trade-offs. But deciding not to have children does, in the long run, limit your family network and the family capital you might have gained otherwise.

If you are married or in a significant relationship, consider how to maintain that relationship and create stability. The presupposition is that you did your homework before marrying or entering the relationship. In the case of Robert, though, he clearly didn't recognize that his future wife Helen would not play the role of mother to his children, which led to their divorce. In chapter 8 I'll review how premarital counseling, counseling for cohabiting couples, and strengthening marriage or relationship programs can help improve the chances for a stable relationship and avoid the type of situation Robert faced.

Understand that finding a partner with similar goals and values has been shown to be key to a successful relationship. Furthermore, the ability of your partner (and yourself) to make and keep commitments is critical in forming a stable relationship. If a potential partner engages in physical or emotional abuse or has a substance abuse problem, run as fast as you can! Although people can change, you may very well be in for trouble in your relationship. Cherlin's advice to take it slow when looking for a partner is particularly apt for those who want a stable, long-term relationship.

Whereas finding the right partner is a key to success, being the right partner is just as important. My clients who have succeeded in their relationships have been willing to sacrifice for their partners and have attempted to meet their partner's needs, rather than focusing on their own needs.

Finally, consider how to prepare for and manage a change in family structure, as, over time, you may need to adapt. My clients have experienced many of the changes in family structure described in the case studies. I encourage my clients to get individual and/or family counseling when transitioning between structures—particularly when they experience a break-up and become a single parent or create a blended family. The husband of a friend of mine died of a heart attack on a business trip, leaving her with three teenagers at home. To help herself and her children work through issues around his death and develop strategies to cope, they went through intensive counseling for several months after his death. Emotional wounds may need to be healed when you transition from one family structure to another, so social support (often from family) and counseling can smooth the transition.

A role clarification exercise has helped my family business clients who have undergone a major change in their family structure.[9] For the exercise, the couple, who are married or in a significant relationship, are asked what they see as their individual role in the family. The role could include providing an income for the family, preparing meals, doing chores around the house, helping children with homework, transporting children to various activities, or disciplining children. Once those roles are clear, each family member seen as mature enough to understand roles and duties describes their role and then allows other family members to agree or disagree with it. Clarifying expectations between partners is particularly important even before getting married or entering a serious relationship.

Sometimes family members may need some prompting, since they may not understand the family expectations. Other times, some family members may negotiate a role, in the case of a disagreement. For example, in the case of Robert, he and his future wife Helen would have benefited from clarifying their parenting roles before they got married. They might have decided not to get married or adjusted their roles to avoid a divorce.

After a role is clarified, that person then gets to ask family members for any help needed to fulfill that role effectively. Further negotiations may ensue. Then the family should ask that person if any further help could facilitate role fulfillment. Sometimes family members can come up with solutions that the person didn't think of.

This exercise allows all family members to describe and clarify their roles and find possible support from others. Participants should write down each family member's role, along with what family members have agreed to do to help. Furthermore, on a regular basis the family should review their roles and their fulfillment of them, including whether the promised help has been delivered. Adjustments often need to be made to family roles over time, perhaps due to changing circumstances or the maturing of family members. As one might expect, role clarification can generate some uncomfortable feelings; if trust is low and the family has trouble communicating, a skilled counsellor may be needed to assist.

Chapter Takeaways

» As the case studies and research show, the various family types affect family capital differently.

» Those in a seemingly disadvantageous family structure can nevertheless develop family capital.

» The role clarification exercise can help stabilize a family, especially during transition to a new structure.

Notes

1. Debra L. Blackwell, "Family Structure and Children's Health in the United States: Findings from the National Health Interview Survey, 2001–2007," *National Center for Health Statistics* 10 no. 246 (2010): 2.

2. Andrew J. Cherlin, *The Marriage-Go-Round* (New York: Vintage, 2010).

3. Ibid., 12.

4. Annette Lareau, *Unequal Childhoods: Class, Race, and Family Life* (Berkeley: University of California Press, 2003).
   Robert D. Putnam, *Our Kids: The American Dream in Crisis* (New York: Simon and Schuster, 2015).

5. Jeffrey H. Larson. "The Verdict on Cohabitation vs. Marriage," *Marriage and Families* 4 no. 3 (2001), http://marriageandfamilies.byu.edu/issues/2001/January/cohabitation.htm.

6. Wikipedia, s.v. "Divorce of Same-Sex Couples," last modified September 27, 2018, https://en.wikipedia.org/wiki/Divorce_of_same-sex_couples.

7. "32 Shocking Divorce Statistics," McKinley Irvin Family Law, October 30, 2012, https://www.mckinleyirvin.com/Family-Law-Blog/2012/October/32-Shocking-Divorce-Statistics.aspx.

8. Alan J. Hawkins, "Will Legislation to Encourage Premarital Education Strengthen Marriage and Reduce Divorce?" *Journal of Law & Family Studies* 9 no. 1 (2007): 79–99.

9. Gibb Dyer and Jeff H. Dyer, *Beyond Team Building: How to Build High Performing Teens and the Culture to Support Them* (New York: Wiley, 2019).

My parents taught me service—
not by saying, but by doing. That was
my culture, the culture of my family.

Alice Walker, novelist

CHAPTER 4

CULTURAL PATTERNS IN FAMILIES THAT ENCOURAGE OR UNDERMINE FAMILY CAPITAL

n the late 1960s, my father, Bill, had a conversation with one of our neighbors, Herb McLean, about the importance of families and how they functioned. As they discussed how their families differed from one another—how they made decisions, delegated chores for family members, set meal times and so forth—the two of them decided to try an experiment to better understand the differences between the Dyer and McLean families. They would swap one child from each family for a week to let the child experience what it was like to live with another family. Then the two families would get together to discuss the differences reported by the two children and hopefully gain insight into how effectively (or ineffectively) they were functioning as a family. (Bill, always the alert social scientist, tried several experiments like this with our family while I was growing up.) My parents felt that my younger brother, Michael, was expendable for a week, so he was sent to live with the McLeans. We, on the other hand, got Herb Jr.; he was my age, and he got to spend a week in Mike's bed, which was situated next to mine. At the end of the week Mike and Herb Jr. gave their reports. Mike described spending a week with the McLeans:

> Every morning about 6:55 a.m., a bell was hand-rung. I was informed that this bell was the five-minute warning for breakfast. No one was late for breakfast. No bells in the evening, but we all ate together. Mrs. McLean was also good to give me a chore to perform; I think that everyone had chores to perform during the week. . . . I swept the carport and the gutters. At our home I often listened to a record while I studied; I don't know if the McLeans owned a stereo—or if I was too timid to ask—but no one played a record of any kind while I was in the home for a week. Somehow I survived.

Herb gave a fairly different description of what the Dyer home was like. I don't have a direct quote from Herb, but what follows is how I would explain my home growing up. No bells of any kind got us up in the morning—each child was responsible for getting up, eating, and getting ready for school. Because my mother was often ill during my childhood (she had significant back problems and several surgeries), she rarely made breakfast for us. So the Dyer children had to fix a bowl of cereal or stir up an instant-breakfast drink to get the day started. Then it was off to school. After school we sometimes did chores, but there was little thought on our part in helping to keep the house clean—a source of constant irritation for our parents. We'd typically come home and listen to the latest recordings of the Beatles, the Rolling Stones, or the Doors while doing our homework; our family pattern was much more relaxed and less structured than the McLeans.

After listening to the reports from Mike and Herb Jr. and asking a few questions, I think both families left the meeting feeling grateful that they were members of their own family. The McLeans appreciated the structure of their household, while the Dyer children were much more comfortable with their autonomy.

In this chapter, I will examine the kinds of family behaviors and processes reflected in family culture to better understand how the culture can either encourage or undermine family capital. I'll use a number of examples from my consulting clients as well as families I have studied to highlight how different family cultures lead to very different results. While family structure provides the context for the development of family capital, and in many ways is decisive in determining the degree to which family capital can be created and accessed, family culture can mitigate negative impacts of a family's structure or negatively affect a more favorable family structure.

What Is Family Culture?

In general, family culture can be defined as "socially acquired and shared rules of conduct that are manifested in a [family's] artifacts, perspectives, values, and assumptions."[1] That definition is somewhat complex, so let's break it down into its component parts.

Artifacts are the overt manifestations of cultural rules. Physical artifacts could be a family's clothing choices, the state of the rooms in the home, and implements used for work or school. Verbal artifacts are the language and stories shared by a family. Behavioral artifacts are a third type; they are the rituals and common behavior patterns used by a family. Artifacts are the tangible aspects of culture—things that we can hear, see, or touch. For example, in my first visit to Japan I was mystified by the artifacts that accompany the process of entering a traditional Japanese home. To enter the home you approach the sliding door entrance. You then slide the door open, step into what is called the *genkan*—where people take off and leave their shoes before stepping up into the home—and then you shout *"gomen kudasai"* and hope that someone comes to the entrance of the home to greet you. If no one comes, you exit the *genkan,* shut the door, and go on your way. In America, if I were to open someone's door, step in, and shout something, I would likely be greeted with an angry homeowner wielding a baseball bat—or worse. So, to understand the Japanese culture, I had to understand the rules of conduct attached to the physical artifacts of the door and the genkan, the behavioral artifacts of walking into the genkan and shouting, and the verbal artifact—the words "*gomen kudasai.*"

Cultural *perspectives* are situation-specific rules of conduct deemed appropriate. For example, in a specific situation like greeting someone in Japan the appropriate behavior is to bow. In the United States and most of the Western world, we shake hands. In the context of a family, perspectives are the situation-specific rules for dealing with things like greeting family members, deciding rules (like curfews), or showing physical affection in public. In my home, my father used to kiss his children (even the boys) on the lips before leaving on a trip—that was deemed appropriate behavior in the Dyer household in that situation. I always assumed that this was due to some Welsh tradition, since his father (my grandfather Will Dyer) was born in Wales. Those outside my family might see such behavior as odd.

Cultural *values* are more general, trans-situational rules that are reflected in cultural perspectives and artifacts. For example, some homes have numerous rules about religious observance: the children are expected to attend Sunday worship service, to say their prayers on a regular basis, and to participate in church service and church recreational activities. These rules in a family could be summarized in a value that might be labelled "religiosity"; in other words, religious observance is important for the family. Other values that I've seen in my consulting include "respect for elders," "honesty in all our dealings," and "hard work is expected." These values are often articulated by members of the family, and these values serve as guides to their actions.

The most fundamental aspects of culture are called *basic assumptions,* or the basic beliefs that underlie the artifacts, perspectives, and values of the family. These assumptions, often unspoken and generally invisible, account for the more overt aspects of culture. To illustrate how these basic assumptions shape a culture, anthropologist Clyde Kluckhohn gives an example from the Navaho tribe of the American Southwest:

> Experience shows that if one asks Navaho Indians about witchcraft, more than 70 percent will give almost identical verbal responses. The replies will vary only in this fashion: "Who told you to talk to me about witchcraft?" "Who said that I knew anything about witchcraft?" "Why do you come to ask about this—who told you I know about it?" . . . Navaho are uniformly careful to hide their faces and to make sure that no other person obtains possession of their hair, nails, spit, or any other bodily part or product. They are likewise characteristically secretive about their personal names. All three of these patterns . . . are manifestations of a cultural . . . premise: "fear of the malevolent activities of other persons." . . . This principle does order all sorts of concrete Navaho behavior and, although implicit, is as much a part of culture as the explicit acts and the verbal symbols.[2]

Thus, in the case of the Navaho that Kluckhohn studied, their basic assumption that others are not to be trusted shaped many of their culture's artifacts, perspectives, and values.

The example of entering a Japanese home versus an American home showed the differences in the cultural artifacts between the two countries. However, ironically, the basic premise underlying those behaviors in the two countries is actually the same: In Japan, people are assumed to still be outside the house while standing in the genkan— even if they are inside the door. In the United States, opening the door without permission symbolizes a violation of the homeowner's space. The underlying assumption about what constituted the homeowner's space is the same in both cultures. If I were to step into the home from the genkan without permission, the Japanese would have been just as upset as Americans would be if I had entered the front door without knocking.

Previous studies of cultural assumptions have suggested several categories that are common to many groups; I've found the following categories of assumptions particularly applicable to families and their ability to develop and transfer family capital:[3]

> » *Assumptions about human nature:* Are people basically good, basically evil, or neither? In other words, can other family members be trusted?
> » *Assumptions about relationships:* Are relationships in the family assumed to be hierarchical (someone is always above someone else in the pecking order), collateral (more or less equal in nature), or individualistic (it's everyone for themselves)?
> » *Assumptions about the environment:* Do we assume that the environment—the physical and social world we live in—can be tamed and shaped by us, do we assume that we are victims of a world we can't change, or are we supposed to harmonize—be one—with our environment?
> » *Assumptions about truth:* Do we learn "truth" from external authority figures or do we gain knowledge and truth through personal investigation and testing?
> » *Assumptions about the nature of human activity:* Do we assume that family members are valuable for what they can do for us or do we see them as individuals with unlimited potential that need to be developed in their own right?
> » *Assumptions about time:* Should we be primarily focused on following the past, living in the present, or preparing for the future?

Where Do Assumptions Come From?

Professor Edgar Schein of MIT, with whom I worked closely for several years as a research assistant, has done extensive study and theorizing regarding the origins of cultural assumptions.[4] He argues that these assumptions are developed as a group (or family) attempts to manage two basic problems of human existence: how to adapt to the environment so the group can survive and thrive, and how to work cooperatively to achieve the group's goals. Schein provides numerous examples of how various groups attempt to solve these two challenges and how they come to a consensus about what works. A group or family's solutions have embedded within them the core assumptions. Thus Schein writes, "Both of these areas of group functioning (adapting to the environment and cooperation) will reflect the macro-cultural context in which the group [or family] exists and from which are derived broader and deeper basic assumptions."[5] Once a family develops its approach to adaptation issues (such as obtaining food and shelter, creating basic security, and protecting its assets) and resolves integration issues (such as helping one another, communicating with family members, and resolving conflicts), the family sees certain actions as the "right way" to do things. These actions and the beliefs attached to them are then passed on to future generations. However, in most cases the future generation is not privy to events that caused the family to adopt certain artifacts, perspectives, values, and their attendant assumptions. For example, my siblings and I never knew why my father kissed us on the lips before leaving on an extended trip. We just accepted it as what was done in the household. I believe the practice had to do with my father's (and the Dyer family's) basic assumption that we love, support, and trust each other, which can be demonstrated physically in the form of a kiss from the father.

Cultural Assumptions as the Foundation of Culture

The listed categories of assumptions suggest a number of ways a family can see themselves, others, and the world around them. To understand culture we must discover the *pattern* of assumptions that forms the foundation of a culture and give rise to certain artifacts, perspectives, and values. Family members enhance family capital when they acquire human, social, and financial capital from their environment, develop such capital themselves, preserve the capital for themselves and future generations, and share that capital with other members in the family. So, for family members to be successful, the family's culture needs to foster enhancement of family capital. In my research I have been able to identify what type of family cultural patterns lead to family-firm continuity and success and which ones lead to dissolution and failure. The following table describes the patterns of assumptions that tend to be associated with the successful acquisition, development, preservation, and sharing of family capital, in addition to the cultural patterns that tend to undermine family capital formation and sharing.

Table 4.1 Cultural Patterns in Families that Encourage and Discourage the Formation and Transfer of Family Capital

Type of Assumption	Assumptions Favoring Family Capital Formation	Assumptions Undermining Family Capital
Human Nature	Family members are trustworthy	Family members can't be trusted
Relationships	Hierarchical → Equal	Individualistic
Environment	Environment can be affected	Environment can't be changed
Truth	Truth is found in family authority figures → Personal investigation	Truth found in family authority figures
Human Activity	Family members can and should be developed	Family members are to be exploited for gain
Time	Past and future oriented	Present oriented

The assumptions in table 4.1 are related to the adaptation and cooperation problems all families face. In particular, the assumptions regarding the environment, truth, human activity, and time are related to helping the family adapt successfully to changing conditions.

Assumptions regarding human nature and relationships focus primarily on the problem of how to cooperate within the family.

Assumptions Affecting Family Integration and Collaboration

The Marriott family, owners and managers of the Marriott Hotel chain, exemplify success in developing family capital through trusting family relationships. The company, founded by Willard and Alice Marriott, has grown substantially over time to be one of the largest hotel chains in the world. In Willard Marriott's biography is a letter he penned to his son and successor, Bill Jr., that notes the kind of trust and relationship they had developed. Here is part of the letter:[6]

Dear Bill,

I am mighty proud of you. Years of preparation, work, and study have shown results.

A leader should have character, be an example in all things. This is his greatest influence. In this you are admirable. You have not taken advantage of your position as my son. You remain humble.

You have proved you can manage people and get them to work for you. You have made a profit—your thinker works. You are developing more patience and understanding with people, more maturity.

It is not often that a father has a son who can step into his shoes and wear them on the basis of his own accomplishments and ability. Being the operating manager of a business on which probably 30,000 people depend for a livelihood is a frightening responsibility, but I have the greatest confidence you will build a team that will ensure the continued success of a business that has been born through years of toil and devotion by many wonderful people . . .

Love and best wishes,

Sincerely,

Dad

This letter reflects the confidence and trust that Willard had in his son Bill. I have consulted with and studied other families with a similar cultural pattern that encourages love and support.

In contrast, the DuPont family, owners of DuPont Chemical Company, regularly ended up suing other family members when conflicts arose because of distrust. Likewise, another family leader interviewed by my research team noted the following:

> I have a son who works for me, but he really doesn't work hard. He's unwilling to make the commitment. He is a good technician, but at this point in my life, I'm unwilling to leave the business to him for this reason: It would destroy him, more than it has already. My business makes a lot of money, and if he were to be in a position to get that kind of income with no investment and no personal commitment, it wouldn't do him any good. It would be the ultimate destruction of him. Maybe not physically, but there would be no growth, no development, no nothing.[7]

The feelings of this father contrast with the confidence and trust Willard Marriott had in his son.

One of my consulting clients also had a significant problem trusting members of his family who worked in his business. Several years ago, Frank (not his real name) called me on the phone with some distressing news: he had found out that at least one of his employees was using a company phone to contact a sex-talk hotline. He felt that whoever was doing this was clearly stealing from the company and engaging in what he considered immoral conduct. As I was leaving on vacation, I told Frank to not do anything until I got back; then, I'd help him think through his options. Two weeks later, after I returned from vacation, I called Frank and was horrified when he said, "I was so upset that I couldn't wait for you to get back from your vacation. I decided that most of the people I was talking to about using the sex-talk hotline were lying to me, so I decided to call my friend who is a polygraph expert. He encouraged me to test those employees who I felt weren't telling me the whole truth with a lie detector. So I checked with my lawyer and eventually decided it was the right thing to do. The first person who I decided to test was my son-in-law who works in the business."[8]

As a result, the son-in-law became so upset that he left the business and filed suit against Frank for invasion of privacy. The son-in-law eventually won a $20,000 judgment against Frank. Over time, Frank's other children left the business, largely due to his distrust of them.

This example of mistrust is extreme; a more common problem is that of "helicopter parents" who attempt to regulate every aspect of their children's lives. Such control reflects an underlying distrust of a child's ability to make independent decisions and thus makes it difficult for the child to develop the self-confidence needed to become a healthy, functioning adult.

Assumptions underpinning relationships are important in the creation and transfer of family capital. In table 4.1 an arrow exists between the terms "hierarchical" and "equal." The arrow signifies that within a family, particularly between parents and children, relationships initially assumed to be hierarchical should evolve to be more egalitarian. Young children are typically in a dependent relationship with their parents, relying on them for guidance and sustenance. However, as the children mature and develop, they can provide help and support to their parents and potentially other family members as well. In the case of Willard Marriott and his son Bill, Willard provided Bill with a set of principles he believed were important to run the Marriott Corporation and for life in general. Some of these principles, passed on to Bill when Willard wrote the letter, are as follows:

» Keep physically fit and mentally and spiritually strong.
» Guard your habits—bad ones will destroy you.
» Pray about every difficult problem.
» Don't criticize people, but make a fair appraisal of their qualifications.
» See the good in people and try to develop those qualities.
» Delegate and hold others accountable for results.

> » Encourage all management to think about better ways and to give suggestions on anything that will improve the business.
> » Think objectively and keep a sense of humor. Make the business fun for you and others.[9]

Whereas initially Bill was dependent upon Willard for support and advice, he eventually developed knowledge and expertise in how to grow a business rapidly. Willard came to trust Bill's judgment on such things, thus creating an *interdependent* relationship in which they learned from and collaborated with each other. While Willard supplied the company vision and values needed for the business to succeed, Bill supplied the financial knowledge and skills to grow the business. They thus developed additional family capital that benefited the Marriott Corporation. Relationships that remain hierarchical keep family members dependent, which stifles development of family members and undermines potential synergy.

In contrast to egalitarian relationships are individualistic relationships, in which self-interest rules supreme. Several scholars have tracked the assumptions underlying marriage over the centuries and suggest that marriage relationships are now primarily based on self-interest.[10] Before the latter part of the nineteenth century, most marriages were based on economic criteria—both men and women wanting to marry someone who would enhance the economic outlook and status of their entire family in society. However, in the latter part of the nineteenth century, around the time the writings of Jane Austen and other authors extolling the virtues of romance gained popularity, love emerged as the criterion for marriage. (As the father of six daughters, I can attest to the power of the writings, as my daughters loved to watch the movies *Pride and Prejudice* and *Sense and Sensibility,* based on Austen's novels.) In recent years, however, the notion that the institution of marriage/cohabitation should primarily serve individual sexual, social, emotional, and economic needs has prevailed; when those needs are not overtly met, divorce or dissolution of the relationship becomes appropriate. Unsurprisingly, the divorce rate has increased in the United States and other countries.

Individualism often trickles down to parent-child and sibling relationships. One example is the Shoen family. Leonard Shoen founded
U-Haul and was married and divorced several times. His children,
who worked in or owned stock in U-Haul, couldn't ever get along.
Relationships got so bad that a fight broke out at a company board
meeting; it was reported in the newspaper:

> A fistfight erupted at a recent U-Haul stockholders' meeting,
> punctuating a bitter family struggle over control of the rental
> empire. Witnesses said the fight Saturday involved the four
> sons of U-Haul founder Leonard Shoen, 73. . . . Two of the
> sons involved in the fight, Mike and Sam, supported their
> father's position in the ownership struggle, while the other
> two, current board chairman Joe and Mark, oppose it. . . .
> Hotel security guards quickly responded to the fight and broke
> it up. Sam Shoen, who was forced to hold an ice pack to his
> cheek afterward, said the fight occurred after the stockhold-
> ers' meeting adjourned. "They ran it in the most high-handed
> possible fashion even though they knew they had the votes
> they needed to win," Sam said. "They were not willing to allow
> discussion on anything." . . . The elder Shoen contended that
> the company has been devalued under Joe's leadership and no
> longer adheres to its founding principles of customer satisfac-
> tion. [Leonard] Shoen . . . appeared to be visibly shaken by the
> brawl. "I created a monster," he said.[11]

The monster that Leonard created resulted from family members
believing each should be looking out for their own self-interest and
not for the interest of the family as a whole. The case underscores the
concept that distrust drains family capital. In the case of the Schoen
family, financial capital was further diminished through costs associated with various lawsuits. Moreover, accounts such as the news
story certainly tarnished the family reputation and that of other stakeholders connected with the Schoen family. Although self-interest is
a part of every person's make-up, to foster family capital one must

subordinate self-interest for family needs or, better still, align self-interest with family goals and objectives.

Assumptions Affecting the Formation and Preservation of Family Capital

A family's assumptions about the environment, truth, human activity, and time can influence the formation and preservation of family capital. The family may see the environment as hostile and immutable (attempting change is futile) while other families may view their environment as mutable. In the field of psychology, the constructs of external (outside forces control people) and internal (people can influence their environment) locus of control describe behavior.[12] A study that a group of student research assistants and I conducted in Mexico about entrepreneurship training for those classified as "poor" illustrates the concept.[13] The Academy for Creating Enterprise (ACE), founded by Steve and Bette Gibson, was initially designed to help poor individuals in the Philippines. The program proved to be successful there, so the Gibsons started another program in Mexico. They realized many of the young people in their program needed both an understanding of business principles and a change in orientation toward their environment. Many program participants felt relatively helpless because prior individual or family attempts to change their circumstances had proved fruitless. Moreover, they hesitated to start a possibly lucrative business because they were unsure wealth was a worthy goal.

Taking their concerns into account, Steve and Bette developed a curriculum that not only taught business skills but also focused on new values and assignments that encouraged them to change their circumstances. For example, one of the first activities for the students was to find people on the street to accept an object such as a rock or paper clip in exchange for something of equal or greater value. They would then repeat the process until, at the end of five or six hours, they would return to the academy to show the rest of the class what they had eventually traded for—something that usually had significantly more value than a rock or paper clip. This exercise dramatically demonstrated to the students that they could change their world and make a difference.

Overall, the training program made a significant difference to participants. We tracked a control group and the participants for approximately two years after they went through the program; participants had significantly more income than the control group. Moreover, those in the ACE program below the poverty line in Mexico received the greatest benefit, with many moving out of poverty after the training. The program shows that the assumption an individual has about the environment can affect their family capital.

The *nature of truth* can similarly facilitate or undermine the formation of family capital. Psychologist Daryl Bem argues that individuals tend to believe that knowledge can be gained from either external authority figures or personal investigation and testing; they typically use one approach at the expense of the other.[14] Although listening to your parents or other authority figures can prove useful—particularly when you are younger—continuing to do so will cause your resources, and thus family capital, to stagnate, as exploring and being innovative yield new solutions to old problems. For example, one entrepreneur I have studied was involved in his business with his wife and daughter. Although quite successful in the trucking industry initially, he had to close his business after several years due to his inability to adapt to changes in the marketplace. His employees called him "the Supreme Intelligence" behind his back because he made all major decisions in the business and the family. He always believed he knew best and would not take advice from his family or employees. His authoritarian management style alienated his employees and daughter. Thus, turnover among employees was high and eventually his daughter left the company due to conflicts with her father. I have seen many other families follow this pattern, which tends to yield stability in the short-run but inhibits innovation and adaptation in the long term.

In contrast, I consulted with a very large family-founded firm started by two brothers who encouraged both family and the firm's employees to seek their own answers to problems. Employees were encouraged to ask others for advice, but they needed to be proactive. One employee I interviewed told me the following story:

> [There's] a phrase: "do what's right." . . . I don't know if it's apoc-
> ryphal or not, but I was given a story when I was first coming
> aboard that described it. . . . A middle manager who wanted
> to do something . . . made this proposal and was told by his
> boss: "no, you can't do that, that's crazy." And so he pushed
> back. He did what was right. He went to the next guy up, his
> functional boss . . . and he was still told that it was crazy. So
> he went to the next level—the vice president's level, and the
> executive people level—and they told him it was crazy, but
> "do what's right." And then he wound up in the president, Bill
> Henry's, office—really selling his idea and Bill Henry told him
> it was crazy, but "do what's right." That kind of thing is a piece
> of the culture that says "if it's right, you do it, but it better be
> right if you've gone all the way. And if you make it work you'll
> get rewarded for it."[15]

Cultural assumptions are often based on solutions to past problems, not present or future problems. Hence, families with a penchant
for exploration and new ideas generally develop and preserve their
resources more effectively than families who strictly rely on authority
figures.

Another important assumption in families that develop family capital is that family members are important assets to be encouraged and
developed. Guidance and positive support from parents and other relatives and opportunities for family members to gain experiences and
education that helps them to succeed accomplish that. In the case of
my own family, my wife, Theresa, and I have provided opportunities
for our children by having them visit other countries, study overseas,
take music lessons, and receive remedial help when they have struggled at school.

Most important, we have made ourselves available to mentor them
when they have faced significant challenges. We were fortunate that

we had the financial means to provide such support to our children. Other high-profile families such as the Marriotts or the Watson family who ran IBM for many years have also provided many mentoring and developmental opportunities for their children and other family members; this is clearly the case in Donald Trump's family as he has given his children opportunities that others could only dream of. While financial means and opportunities help when parents want to help develop their children, we've seen numerous examples of individuals who, despite humble backgrounds, were given guidance, support, and opportunities that allowed them to rise above their circumstances (a good example is former president of the United States, Barack Obama).

Unfortunately, some families see members as assets to be exploited rather than developed. You need only look at the statistics regarding family violence and abuse to understand the scope of this terrible scourge.[16] Here are just a few of the sobering statistics:

> » In the United States, an average of twenty people are physically abused by intimate partners every minute. That's more than ten million abuse victims annually.
> » One in five women and one in seven men have been severely physically abused by an intimate partner (e.g., assault, rape).
> » One in three female murder victims and one in twenty male murder victims are killed by intimate partners.
> » Seventy-two percent of all murder-suicides are perpetrated by intimate partners and 94 percent of murder victims of murder-suicide are female.
> » In 2015, 683,000 children were either abused or neglected in the United States.[17]

Such violence and abuse often leave long term physical and emotional scars not easily healed, leading to mental health issues for the victims, which are frequently compounded by substance abuse and a continuation of the cycle as they form their own families. Families caught up in a web of abuse and violence are typically unable to generate their own family capital—particularly human capital—that can be passed on to future generations.

An experiment conducted by a professor at Stanford University in the 1960s clarifies the last assumption considered, that of *time*.[18] The experiment consisted of putting four-year-old children in a room with a tasty looking marshmallow. The children were told they could either eat the marshmallow right away or wait fifteen minutes and get two marshmallows. The researcher then left the room and watched the children through a two-way mirror. Seventy percent of the children couldn't wait fifteen minutes; 30 percent had enough impulse control to wait and get the extra marshmallow. The researcher then tracked the children over time and discovered that the children who couldn't wait had more behavioral problems later in life. Those who waited tended to be more optimistic, had higher motivation, earned better grades and incomes, and had healthier relationships. Thus, the ability to delay gratification pays big dividends.

Regarding assumptions about time, families seem to be primarily oriented to the past, the present, or the future. The children who ate the marshmallow had a difficult time envisioning a future with the reward of the extra marshmallow and wanted to be satisfied now. From my experience in Asia, the past is often the anchor for behavior in that part of the world, while in Western countries, the people tend to be more oriented to achieving a new (and hopefully better) future.

In terms of family capital, a strictly present or past orientation tends to lead to the worst outcomes. Families oriented to the past are often unwilling to try different solutions and therefore don't foster much innovation and change that might generate more family capital. Families with a present orientation tend to find themselves in a resource poor environment; when they gain resources they are quick to consume them rather than save or leverage those resources to create a better future. Carol Stack, in her book *All Our Kin*, illustrates how resources are quickly consumed in a poor neighborhood: "When Magnolia and Calvin inherited a sum of money the information quickly spread to every member of their domestic network. Within a month and a half all of the money was absorbed by participants in their network whose demands and needs could not be refused."[19]

When resources are scarce and people don't know if and when they might be available again, the natural tendency will be to quickly consume resources or to share them with family or with those in their social network whom they feel obligated to help. Altruistic behavior is laudable, but it makes saving money and other resources difficult—thus making it more difficult to start a business or invest in other resources or opportunities.

I have consulted with entrepreneurs whose families have been primarily oriented to the past. "That's the way we've always done it" is the typical response to my question concerning a certain practice that I've observed within their family. Whereas relying on past values and practices provides some stability, it also makes envisioning a different—and possibly more effective—way of functioning harder. For example, one family that I worked with from Latin America had fallen into a pattern of verbal and even physical confrontations when they disagreed. I tried to get the family to be more objective and less emotional in handling their disagreements, though I was not very successful. In the end the business suffered and eventually went bankrupt. I couldn't get the family to envision a future where family members cooperated with one another and where the business quickly adapted to changing marketplace conditions.

Families that I've worked with who have been successful in developing family capital seem to actually have a mix of the past and future orientations. They have certain beliefs and practices from the past that they can rely on to help them as they anticipate and solve problems. But they aren't so wedded to the past that they don't look for new, innovative practices that might help in the future. Healthy families are inclined toward action and improvement as they navigate an uncertain and changing world. Thus, in table 4.1, I note that an orientation toward time based on the past *and* the future leads to the successful formation of family capital.

Unfortunately, data from the Economic Policy Institute (EPI) regarding American's retirement savings suggests that Americans are not very future oriented.[20] This is a recipe for financial disaster for many Americans families. The EPI reports:

» Nearly half of all Americans have no retirement savings.
» The median working-age family had only $5,000 in savings. In contrast, the top 1 percent of all families had saved $1,080,000 or more.
» Single men (43 percent) and single women (42 percent) are much less likely to save than married couples (65 percent). Again, being married has advantages.
» Sixty-five percent of whites had a savings account compared with 41 percent of blacks and 26 percent of Hispanics.

Your wealth certainly has a bearing on how much money you can save, but even some of those with wealth are not planning for their retirement. The mantra seems to be "spend today, and let the future take care of itself." Those without a future orientation may need to rely on the government or their family for support in retirement and they will have little or no financial resources to leave to their posterity.

Family Assumptions in Practice

The assumptions underlying the family culture may vary significantly, and some that encourage family capital may pair with assumptions antithetical to family capital. I have seen some families with members who distrust one another and whose relationships are individualistic—yet who also believe that knowledge doesn't reside only in family leaders and that each member needs to individually discover what's true. To determine the assumptions in a given family is no mean feat, for family members are unlikely to clearly articulate those they operate from. Generally, one must examine the artifacts, perspectives, and values of a family to infer the assumptions that underlie them.

Changing Family Culture

What might be done to change a family culture that undermines family capital? The question is difficult to answer since changing culture is not easy. A number of years ago I did several in-depth studies of cultural change in organizations.[21] Change typically occurs when a major company crisis calls into question the effectiveness of the organization's culture, and management is replaced by those with different cultural assumptions and values. Unfortunately, as a researcher and consultant to many families and family businesses, I have noticed that resistance to change is common and that cultural change rarely occurs—families, unlike businesses, can't just fire family members and replace them with others they like better. I have discovered that family culture change generally coincides with the death or disability of the family patriarch/matriarch and with new leadership.

In lieu of such dramatic circumstances, a few approaches may bear fruit. One that I've required with clients is family counseling. Good family counselors encourage family members to examine the assumptions underlying their family's behavior, help the family gain insight regarding the negative outcomes of the family's culture, and then help the family develop a new culture based on new assumptions, values, perspectives, and artifacts that will allow them to function more effectively. The process is difficult and can take months or even years. But it is often the best chance for a family to change its culture for the better.

Another approach is for the family to identify the kinds of assumptions that underlie the family culture. At the end of this chapter is a diagnostic questionnaire that a family could use to identify whether its culture is based on trust versus distrust, hierarchical or more egalitarian relationships, etc. Then the family should examine the more general rules used by the family (their values) and the situation specific rules (perspectives) that tend to cause problems in the family. The family next can make action plans to change their artifacts—behavioral patterns, language, and so forth—to reflect a different set of assumptions (and hopefully get better outcomes). At that point in the process, the family may need an outside consultant or facilitator who will help the members agree on what changes need to be made and then follow up to make sure they follow through. This process can likewise be fraught with difficulty, but has the best chance for success. In my experience, families that experience abuse, distrust, or victimization and helplessness have great difficulty changing their culture without external support and a willingness to explore new beliefs and behaviors.

Chapter Takeaways

» The most fundamental aspect of family culture is its basic assumptions.

» Assumptions that encourage trust, equality and cooperation, proactive behavior, truth-seeking, development of all members, and an orientation toward the future coupled with what works from the past are key to creating family capital.

» Distrust of others, individualistic relationships, a fatalistic attitude toward the environment, an exclusive reliance on others for gaining knowledge, an exploitative attitude toward others, and a focus on the present ruin family capital.

» The Survey of Family Capital Cultural Assumptions provides a basic diagnostic tool for determining whether a family culture encourages family capital.

Survey of Family Capital Cultural Assumptions

Circle the number that best describes where your family might be placed on the following continuum of cultural assumptions. While certain family members may differ along these dimensions, estimate where the family as a whole falls along the continuum:

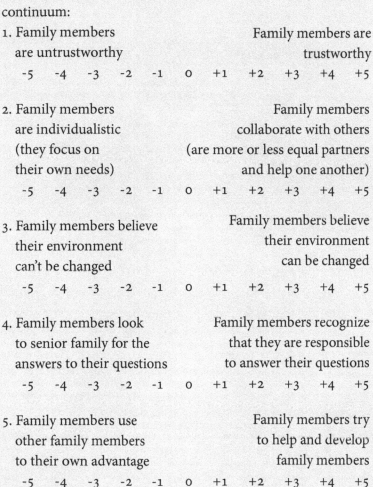

1. Family members are untrustworthy

   Family members are trustworthy

   -5   -4   -3   -2   -1   0   +1   +2   +3   +4   +5

2. Family members are individualistic (they focus on their own needs)

   Family members collaborate with others (are more or less equal partners and help one another)

   -5   -4   -3   -2   -1   0   +1   +2   +3   +4   +5

3. Family members believe their environment can't be changed

   Family members believe their environment can be changed

   -5   -4   -3   -2   -1   0   +1   +2   +3   +4   +5

4. Family members look to senior family for the answers to their questions

   Family members recognize that they are responsible to answer their questions

   -5   -4   -3   -2   -1   0   +1   +2   +3   +4   +5

5. Family members use other family members to their own advantage

   Family members try to help and develop family members

   -5   -4   -3   -2   -1   0   +1   +2   +3   +4   +5

6. Family members   Family members focus on
   focus on the present   preparing for the future

   -5   -4   -3   -2   -1   0   +1   +2   +3   +4   +5

7. Family is a   Family is seen
   low priority   as a high priority

   -5   -4   -3   -2   -1   0   +1   +2   +3   +4   +5

8. Family members spend   Family members
   little time together   spend a great deal
   (including time on the   of time together
   phone, internet, etc.)

   -5   -4   -3   -2   -1   0   +1   +2   +3   +4   +5

Scoring: Now total up the scores for the eight items. The scores could range from -40 to +40.

Families with cultures that foster high levels of family capital generally would score between +30 and +40. Those with more modest means of generating family capital would score between +20 and +30, while those with cultures that encourage some family capital formation would score between +10 and +20. A score between 0 and +10 would indicate only a minimal amount of support for family capital. A negative score would suggest that family capital would have difficulty being creating and sustained. Scores between 0 and -20 would indicate a low likelihood of generating family capital. A score between -20 and -30 would suggest significant problems related to family capital formation, and a score between -30 and -40 would suggest a culture that has a severe family capital deficiency—if not now, certainly in the future.

Notes

1. William G. Dyer, "Cultural Change in Family Firms: Anticipating and Managing Business and Family Transitions," *Admininstrative Science Quarterly* 32 no. 4 (1987): 635.

2. Clyde Kluckhohn, "The Concept of Culture," in *The Policy Sciences,* eds. D. Lerner and H. D. Lasswell (Palo Alto, CA: Stanford University Press, 1951).

3. Dyer, "Cultural Change in Family Firms: Anticipating and Managing Business and Family Transitions."

4. Edgar H. Schein, *Organizational Culture and Leadership* (San Francisco: Jossey-Bass, 2010).

5. Ibid., 18.

6. Robert O'Brien, *Marriott* (Salt Lake City: Deseret Book, 1987), 65.

7. W. Gibb Dyer, *The Entrepreneurial Experience* (San Francisco: Jossey-Bass,1992), 196.

8. Dyer, *The Entrepreneurial Experience,* 102.

9. O'Brien, *Marriott,* 265–267.

10. Andrew Cherlin, *The Marriage-Go-Round: The State of Marriage and the Family in America Today* (New York: Vintage, 2010).
    W. J. Dyer, "Shifting views on the male-female relationship." *The Religious Educator,* 18 (2017): 31-51.

11. "U-Haul Meeting Erupts into a Family Fistfight," *Deseret News,* March 6, 1989, D5.

12. Julian B. Rotter, "Generalized Expectancies for Internal Versus External Control of Reinforcement," *Psychological Monographs: General & Applied* 80 no. 1(1966): 1–28.

13. W. Gibb Dyer et al., "Can the Poor Be Trained to Be Entrepreneurs?: The Case of the Academy for Creating Enterprise in Mexico," *Journal of Developmental Entrepreneurship* 21 no. 2 (2016): 1–22.

14. Daryl J. Bem, *Beliefs, Attitudes, and Human Affairs* (Belmont, CA: Brooks/Cole, 1970).

15. W. Gibb Dyer, "Culture in Organizations: A Case Study and Analysis," *MIT Working Paper* (1982): 27–28.

16. *Domestic Violence Statistics* prepared by the National Coalition Against Domestic Violence.

17. Child Maltreatment 2015 prepared by the Children's Bureau, https://www.acf.hhs.gov/cb/resource/child-maltreatment-2015.

18. Walter Mischel and Ebbe B. Ebbesen October 1970. "Attention in Delay of Gratification," *Journal of Personality and Social Psychology* 16 no. 2 (1970): 329–37.

19. Carol Stack, *All Our Kin* (New York: Basic Books, 1974).

20. Monique Morrissey, "The State of American Retirement," *Economic Policy Institute,* March 3, 2016, https://www.epi.org/publication/retirement-in-america.

21. W. Gibb Dyer Jr., "The Cycle of Cultural Evolution in Organizations" in *Gaining Control of the Corporate Culture,* eds. Ralph Kilmann and Associates (San Francisco: Jossey-Bass, 1985), 200–29.

The most important . . . work that you will ever do will be the work you do within the walls of your own home.

Harold B. Lee, religious leader

CHAPTER 5

FAMILY ACTIVITIES THAT CREATE AND STRENGTHEN FAMILY CAPITAL

Specific activities and practices develop and cement capital within the family. In this chapter I will use examples from my own family, my clients, and research. The "Family Capital Activity Survey" at the end of the chapter will help you determine to what extent your family develops capital through such efforts.

The "Secrets" of Creating Family Capital

Characteristics important for family capital include (1) family identity, (2) family rituals and traditions, (3) commitment to family, (4) coping with crises, and (5) spiritual wellness. These characteristics, strengthened by family activities, create stability within families.

We Are Family—The Role of Family Identity

When working with families who own businesses, I have come to realize that they tend to have family members with personal identities inextricably connected with family identities. Identifying oneself with a family tends to encourage commitment to and resource sharing with the family. Moreover, a strong family identity encourages family members to develop strategies and goals to preserve that family identity.

One family with a strong identity that I consulted with for several years was the Bucksbaum family, owners of General Growth Properties, founded by brothers Martin and Matthew Bucksbaum. Starting with a shopping center in Cedar Rapids, Iowa, in 1954, Martin and Matthew developed shopping centers and malls across the United States. By 2007 they had acquired 194 malls with over 200 million square feet, and the family's combined net worth was over $2 billion (until the financial crisis of 2008). In the early 1990s, I was asked by one of their financial advisors to help them with some concerns they had regarding their management team, and to provide some help and support for John Bucksbaum, Matthew's son, who was the likely successor to the two brothers. (John had a sister, Ann, and Martin had a daughter, Mary, and two stepsons. Neither Ann nor Mary had strong interest in taking over the management of the business, but one of Martin's stepsons had held a leadership role in the company.)

I first met Martin and Matthew in Las Vegas at a convention they were attending. They looked like brothers, and as I worked with Martin and Matthew over several years I came to learn that, like most brothers, they had some disagreements but by and large showed a united front when dealing with many business challenges. Their Jewish heritage was very important to them, and their family's identity was closely connected to their faith as well as their business. Being a Bucksbaum meant something—it identified them, both in the business and in the community.

Philanthropy has also been a cornerstone of the Bucksbaum family and its identity. The family has given of their wealth to many organizations to enrich the communities they lived in (mostly Iowa and Chicago). For example, Matthew and his wife Carolyn donated $42 million to the University of Chicago to create the Bucksbaum Institute for Clinical Excellence, and the family has provided strong support to Aspen Music Festival, the Chicago Symphony, and the Lyric Opera of Chicago. Matthew also served his faith as president of the Temple B'nai Jeshurun. In meetings with Martin and Matthew and in the long conversations that I had with John it was clear that the Bucksbaum family wanted to leave a positive legacy in their communities. They saw themselves as being distinct from other families. They wanted to be known for exemplifying hard work, well-designed shopping malls, integrity, and service to their communities.

Other families I have worked with have had similar intentions to create a clear family identity. One such is the family of Stephen Covey, author of *The Seven Habits of Highly Effective People.* Covey was a member of the Department of Organizational Behavior at Brigham Young University when I was a student there, and I served as his teaching assistant for one semester. He also attended one of my family business workshops (he involved his family in his consulting business) and wrote an endorsement for one of my books, so I got to know Steve quite well. One way Steve strengthened his family was by creating a family mission statement. Steve wrote the following about family mission statements: "Write a family mission statement—identify what kind of family you want to be. For instance, what qualities define your family, what kinds of feeling(s) do you want in your home, how do you want to build relationships? Get everyone involved in these questions and write something that describes your family and how you want to be."[1]

Some families keep a family shield or crest with symbolic meaning that differentiates their family from others. I remember when my parents took all of their children and grandchildren on a family vacation to Southern California, and all family members were supplied with (and were required to wear) a T-shirt with the family name on it. Now that's one way to set a family apart from others.

As I thought about creating a family mission statement, I asked myself what being a Dyer meant. Several core values or beliefs came to mind. Here are a few:

> » We remember our roots—we're descendants of poor immigrants from Europe. We treat everyone equally and with respect.
> » Family comes first. We treat each other with love and respect.
> » Hugs are good.
> » We work hard and play hard.
> » We enjoy sports, music, the arts, and other culturally uplifting activities.
> » Knowledge is power, so we encourage education and learning. Travel is often the best teacher.

I shared these (and other) "Dyer values" with my siblings, children, grandchildren, and extended family at a recent family party and asked if they agreed or disagreed with the points and if they could think of others. We are currently in the process of finalizing a statement of "Dyer values," which I hope will help foster unity and help pass our values to future generations.

Oral and written histories or journals also reinforce the uniqueness of a family. My father and I have written personal histories, in which we describe many successes and failures and how we coped with challenges. These experiences will hopefully encourage progeny when they face hard times and get them to realize that their progenitors weren't perfect. My great-grandfather John Lye Gibb was fortunate to have a biography written about him that has been shared within the family. Histories and historical events ground the family and are a point of reference from which family members view the world and each other. They give family members a sense of belonging and community that encourages them to connect with and help one another.

My father was a great storyteller. He often told stories to illustrate an important value he thought his children should emulate. The following story, about Nastromus, the architect of a lighthouse in Alexandria, Egypt, was one of our favorites:

Once upon a time there was a king in Egypt named Philip—a proud and haughty king—who decided toward the end of his life to leave a memorial to himself. He determined that he would build a beacon tower on the banks of the Nile River that would shine its light to travelers by water and by land. In the foundation stone of the tower he would put his name and the workings of his kingdom. He commissioned an architect named Nastromus to supervise the construction of the edifice and then promptly forgot about the commission. But Nastromus drew up the plans, hired the workmen, gathered the materials, and supervised the construction of the building.

As the lighthouse neared completion, Nastromus began to think to himself about his situation. He concluded that it was he and not the king who was the real builder of the lighthouse and he should receive the enduring credit and fame. So he devised a secret plan. One night he had the workmen chisel his name into the foundation stone of the lighthouse. Over that he placed a thin veneer of rock, and on that facade he inscribed the name of King Philip and the workings of his kingdom. When the lighthouse was dedicated, the people came and gave acclaim and praise to the king. After the king died and as the years went by, the winds and the rains and the elements beat upon the lighthouse and began to erode away the thin veneer of the rock. Then one morning, after a storm, the people saw that the facade had been washed away. There was the name "Nastromus, the architect," revealed to stand for as long as the lighthouse should stand, engraved in the foundation stone.

I don't know if this story is actually true. Regardless, Bill used it to stress that we can display any facade we wish, but a time will come when we will be unmasked, to stand as the true builders of our personal lighthouses. Thus our actions should be congruent with our beliefs. To Bill, hypocrisy was a mortal sin and with this story he hoped to make that belief part of the family identity.

Families can further identify themselves by sharing pictures, events, feelings, and anecdotes on social media and blogs. Many families, including my own, keep track of other family members that way. We also keep scrapbooks with pictures of family members and family events and have created picture books of vacations or other family outings, using Shutterfly or other such firms. We have converted old eight-millimeter family movies and slides to a digital format that we watch periodically. They remind us of earlier times and promote good feelings toward one another and what we have done together.

Family Rituals and Traditions

Family rituals and traditions play a significant role in creating familial bonds. Rituals and traditions of the Dyer family distinguish us from other families. Here are a few:

» Vacations to the beach in Oregon to go crabbing and clamming.
» Vacations to Cedar City, Utah, to see Shakespeare's plays and go fishing.
» A special Christmas Day breakfast of finnan haddie (smoked cod) and "Robbs" (scones named after the Robb family).
» A Christmas Eve presentation by the children, consisting of opening one present and reenacting the Christmas story of Jesus Christ's birth—in costume.
» The Dyer family Christmas party. My brother Michael creates a new "Dyer family poem" each year that he reads. The poem, typically patterned after a Dr. Seuss rhyming scheme, includes some funny things that happened to family members during the past year.
» The Dyer family Halloween party. We all dress up, play games, and eat.
» Regular family dinners.
» Regular family nights when the family prays, sings, teaches about family and moral values, and plays games.
» Trips with the grandchildren to Disneyland.

» Visits to our ancestors' graves on Memorial Day.
» A family picture on Dyer Street in Lake Oswego, Oregon under the street sign. (This is the street where my grandfather supposedly lived while growing up.)

These traditions represent a mix of traditions from both Theresa's family and my own. We have kept many of the traditions from both the Franck family and the Dyer family, but I chose not to keep one tradition. I felt a little uncomfortable with the previously mentioned kissing tradition of my father for some reason and decided not to continue it with my son, Justin. As families evolve, they need to decide which family rituals and traditions to keep and which to abandon.

Demonstrating Commitment

Families with capital emphasize the importance of spending time with family members and demonstrating commitment to the family. Since most of my clients are entrepreneurs, this isn't easy given the pressures to achieve in business. One survey of entrepreneurs noted that 82 percent of entrepreneurs who had been in business for less than five years worked most evenings.[2] Additionally, 70 percent of those who had been in business between six and ten years worked evenings, while 58 percent of those who had been in business for ten or more years were frequently gone at night.[3] One entrepreneur reported to me that early in his career he found it challenging to find time for work and family until his wife gave him an ultimatum: be at home for dinner each night by 7:00 p.m.—or else. Though the ultimatum introduced complexity, the commitment he made helped him to build relationships with his children and provided a sense of stability and certainty. Current research shows that those families that share evening meals function more effectively and develop better relationships than those families who don't.[4] Given the pressures and needs of work and family, families need to be creative to find time together. One entrepreneur expressed frustrations and regrets: "My wife is very supportive but occasionally has to demand my attention. She gets fed up with me being gone all night, especially this spring when I was traveling so much. It was very hard on her. It has been stressful in a lot of ways."[5] Another lamented, "I've always had a problem finding time for my family. I overdid it on the work side—I should have spent more time with my family."[6]

The time we spend with family reflects our commitment to family members. A seminal study of 3,000 families conducted by Nick Stinnett and John DeFrain noted that commitment to family was the first "secret" of a strong family.[7] They tell the story of one man who was saved as a child when his mother dove in front of an automobile and pushed him out of the way. Such an act clearly reflected the mother's love and commitment to her child and left an indelible impression on the son. While such heroic acts are compelling, simpler acts such as taking family vacations, going to the park, attending children's sporting or cultural activities, and having regular family dinners demonstrate the commitment that family members have for each other.

Without family time and commitment, family capital may not be adequately nurtured. Christian Smith, a sociologist at the University of Notre Dame and an expert on American families, clearly articulates the problems of finding time for and showing commitment to family in his book *Soul Searching*:

> Although many Americans talk about what a pro-family, youth-loving society ours is, it is not entirely clear that many of our actual practices and institutions support those claims. Most of the structures and routines of American life actually pull families apart regularly and effectively. American work and education practices separate family members for most daytime hours of every weekday. Day care centers and preschools remove children from their parents at a very young age. After school, many parents, middle-class parents particularly, schedule their children's lives with so many programmed activities that they find themselves with very little unstructured time simply to spend together as families. A minority of American families [about one-third] with teenagers eat most

of their meals together. And our legal system and cultural practices around divorce make clear that keeping families together is not a particularly high societal priority. Contrary to our culture's pro-family rhetoric, an alien anthropologist might have good reason to conclude that members of American families actually have little interest in spending time together. To be clear, the point here is not that individual parents and other adults are rotten people who do not love their children. These, rather, are largely matters of routine cultural practices and institutional structures from which it is very difficult to deviate. But they do send messages to and have consequences for the youth of our society.[8]

When parents don't spend time mentoring their children, the children may be like rudderless ships tossed about by society's winds blowing from all directions. And without a way to navigate the storm, children can become directionless and have difficulty creating meaningful, productive lives. Families that spend time together have better results.

My consulting work bears that out. A number of years ago I was on a conference panel with Peter Huntsman, the current CEO of Huntsman Chemical and son of the well-known industrialist Jon Huntsman. Peter remembered his father being very busy as he was growing up but noted that he particularly enjoyed trips with his father to visit various company factories during his teenage years. Peter said he was often given the opportunity to say a few words to Huntsman employees after his father had given a speech or presentation. So even a busy father like Jon Huntsman felt it was important to mentor his son by bringing him along on certain business trips. One cannot overestimate the power of example when a child spends time with his or her parents.

While I was growing up, my father often left for academic conferences or consulting assignments. However, when he was home he had a strategy to spend time with his children that paid dividends: fishing. Bill was a great storyteller, and what better way to get a captive audience than by renting a boat and spending several hours alone with his children on a lake. He was a good fisherman who taught us how to catch fish (we generally caught quite a few, making the experience enjoyable), but he also told us stories, answered questions, and created bonds of trust and reciprocity. Following my father's lead, I've continued this fishing tradition with my own children and grandchildren. Similar activities can do much to build family capital.

Coping with Crises

Stinnett and DeFrain noted in their study that strong families have the ability to cope with significant family crises. I have found that to be true in the families that I have studied and worked with. One such family was the Raymond family of Greene, New York. I met the family patriarch, George Raymond, in the early 1980s as I began a research project at the Raymond Corporation. As with all my clients, I initially spent a couple hours getting to know him by asking about the family and its history. In George's case, the Raymond Corporation was founded by his father, George Raymond Sr., and George took over leadership of the business when his father retired. George grew up in Greene and married a local girl named Cynthia "Cynnie" Spencer. They had three children: George III (who liked to be called "Pete"), Steve, and Jean. His story seemed fairly similar to that of some other clients until he described the events of June 1, 1977.

George came home from work that day only to find two bags of groceries on the floor and Cynthia gone. George couldn't believe she'd leave groceries on the floor, and as he searched the house he found several things amiss. As he looked outside, he saw that the telephone lines were cut. He immediately called the police, who, after a few hours of investigation, determined Cynthia had been kidnapped. After several days of searching, the police found Cynthia's body in the woods many miles from home—she'd been killed by a deranged Vietnam veteran. The man had kidnapped Cynthia with the idea that he would eventually come forward and "solve" her kidnapping and murder; as a result, he would be given the job of police chief in a nearby town. George, his children, Raymond Corportation employees, and the community were devastated by Cynthia's death. In dealing with this traumatic event, George later wrote:

> Before Cynnie's death if anyone had asked me what kind of father I'd been, I would have said a good one. I tried to emulate with my children the relationship I'd had with my own father. I thought he would be a good model, a fine standard to shoot for. I did the best I could and, frankly, I thought I'd done pretty well. But the violent death of their mother at age fifty-five had a devastating effect on our kids. Looking back, I would say that the boys recovered fairly well, and, all things considered, relatively quickly, but it took Jean ten long, hard years, and even to this day I think she bears the scars of that horrid day in June.[9]

During the course of my initial interview and in subsequent conversations, George talked about the social support he and his children received from family, friends, and Raymond employees when Cynthia died and how George and his children had learned to support each other during this difficult time. I also interviewed Pete, Steve, and Jean. Consistent with what George reported, I could see that whereas all the children had suffered from Cynthia's untimely death, her passing had a much deeper and profound effect on Jean. Although the Raymond children had experienced significant trauma related to their mother's death, they had—on the whole—become successful adults and were functioning well. George eventually remarried, which created its own unique set of problems for the family, but the Raymonds were able to pull together during the crisis of Cynthia's death and help each other get through it.

In my own family a major crisis occurred after my daughter Emily and her husband, Burke, adopted a beautiful baby girl named Evelyn. Evelyn was small at birth and developed what is called "failure to thrive" syndrome—she was very small and quite weak. Only breastmilk from generous nursing mother donors was able to keep her alive. Unfortunately, we were to discover that her failure to thrive was only the start of her medical problems. Three months after her birth she was rushed by ambulance to Primary Children's Hospital in Salt Lake City with what was thought to be a serious infection. Theresa and I hurried to the hospital to find Emily and Burke in the emergency room holding Evelyn in what appeared to be an almost comatose state. After a series of tests we learned Evelyn had a condition called hemophagocytic lymphohistiocytosis (HLH), a very rare condition caused by one's immune system running wild, generating lymphocytes and macrophages that produce high amounts of inflammatory cytokines, which damage vital organs. Without treatment, it is invariably fatal. The only cure for Evelyn would be chemotherapy followed by a bone marrow transplant. For the next year, from February 2009 until the spring of 2010, Evelyn was in and out of the hospital (mostly in), and one of her parents stayed with her the entire time. Family members, particularly my wife Theresa, would periodically go to the hospital to tend Evelyn and give Emily or Burke a well-deserved break. After enduring chemotherapy and finding a matching bone marrow donor in Germany, Evelyn experienced a successful transplant and, as of this writing, is a healthy and happy ten-year-old. Without the expertise of those doctors and nurses, Evelyn would not have survived; but the social support given by the family to Evelyn and her parents was as important—if not more important—in helping the family cope. Moreover, as the result of successfully weathering this storm, our family became closer. Adversity, rather than pulling a family apart, can strengthen a family and enhance its capital.

Unfortunately, not all families weather a crisis well. Crises inevitably bring tension and stress that can undermine relationships. Some families that I have worked with have crumbled under the pressure of a crisis they were unable to cope with—the result often being a divorce or the estrangement of family members.

Spiritual Wellness—Achieving a Higher Purpose

Stinnett and DeFrain describe the characteristic of spiritual wellness, which means the family engages in a purpose transcending family members merely living together as a biological or economic unit. They write, "[Spiritual wellness is] a unifying force, a caring center within each person that promotes sharing, love, and a compassion for others. It is a force that helps a person transcend self and become part of something larger."[10] Some families, like the Bucksbaums, follow values espoused by their religion. That entails leading a life consistent with your religious values and typically involves some sort of service to others—particularly those in need. The Bucksbaum family has been devoted to the values of the Jewish tradition—attending synagogue, and participating in Jewish traditions—which has helped the family develop its identity and clarify the values on which the family culture is based. Religious observance by a family like the Bucksbaums encourages family members to spend meaningful time together and creates opportunities for the family to discuss those important values and beliefs. Furthermore, their philanthropic activity strengthens family relationships and encourages family members to achieve a higher purpose in life.

Families not religiously inclined can also achieve spiritual wellness. I have seen families with little or no religious affiliation sponsor relief activities for the poor in developing countries or service projects in their local community. Paradoxically, they strengthen their own family by going outside the family to help others. The key to developing this higher purpose is for the family to clearly identify how its members can contribute to society in a meaningful way. Discussions within the family at a "family council" or developing a mission statement that articulates the family's beliefs and values as they relate to service and achieving a higher purpose could accomplish that.

Chapter Takeaways

» Family activities, rituals, and traditions bond family members and contribute to family capital.
» Making commitments to family, coping well with crises, and creating a sense of spiritual wellness likewise bring family together and add to their capital.

Family Capital Activity Survey

1. Does your family have a formal or informal mission statement or understanding of "who we are" and "what we stand for"?
   Yes   No

2. Does your family have regular meals together?
   Yes   No

3. Does your family have periodic family councils or family nights to discuss family issues and concerns?
   Yes   No

4. Does your family have traditions and/or rituals that you observe on a regular basis?
   Yes   No

5. Does your family regularly communicate via phone, email, Facebook, Twitter, or other social media?
   Yes   No

6. Does your family have family videos, pictures, or scrapbooks that highlight the importance of family and family events?
   Yes   No

7. Does your family have written family histories, diaries, or journals?
   Yes   No

8. Does your family share "family stories" about important events in the family's history?
   Yes   No

9. Does your family have regular activities—picnics, vacations, camping, etc.—that family members participate in?
   Yes   No

10. Does your family regularly attend church together or participate in other activities to promote "spiritual wellness"?

Yes   No

11. Do family members generally attend events where other family members are performing (e.g., sports, music, plays, etc.)?

Yes   No

12. Do family members generally come to each other's aid when facing a crisis or serious problem?

Yes   No

13. Do family members feel that they spend enough time together?

Yes   No

14. Do family members feel a strong commitment to the family?

Yes   No

Scoring: If you had 10 or more "yes" answers, then your family is likely doing well in developing family capital. Scores of 7 to 9 would indicate "moderate" success in developing family capital, while scores of 6 or lower would indicate that your family is probably having some difficulty in developing family capital.

Notes

1. "The Seven Habits of Highly Effective People," Franklin Covey, http://www.stephencovey.com/blog/?tag=family-mission-statement.

2. David P. Boyd and David E. Gumpert, "The Effects of Stress on Early Age Entrepreneurs," in *Frontiers of Entrepreneurship Research*, eds. John A. Hornaday, Jeffry A. Timmons, and Karl H. Vesper (Babson Park, MA: Babson College, 1983) 180–191.

3. Ibid., 180–191.

4. Christian Smith, *Soul Searching: The Religious and Spiritual Lives of American Teenagers* (Oxford: Oxford University Press, 2005).

5. Jeffrey H. Dyer, *The Entrepreneurial Experience: Confronting Career Dilemmas of the Start-Up Executive* (San Francisco: Jossey-Bass, 1992), 77.

6. Ibid., 77.

7. Nick Stinnett and John DeFrain, *The Secrets of Strong Families* (Boston: Little, Brown, 1985).

8. Christian Smith, *Soul Searching: The Religious and Spiritual Lives of American Teenagers*, 190.

9. George G. Raymond, *All in the Family Business* (Chevy Chase, MD: Posterity Press, 2001), 148.

10. Stinnett and DeFrain, *The Secrets of Strong Families*, 101.

Family is a unique gift that needs to be appreciated and treasured, even when they're driving you crazy. As much as they make you mad, interrupt you, annoy you, curse at you, try to control you, these are the people who know you the best and who love you.

Jenna Morasca, actress

CHAPTER 6

BUILDING TRUST: THE FOUNDATION OF FAMILY CAPITAL

All families have their secrets. To illustrate the importance of trust, I'm going to share a secret from my own family.

My uncle Jack Gibb was born on December 20, 1914, but the events surrounding his nativity are shrouded in mystery. My grandmother Ada evidently had a boyfriend, but her father, John Lye Gibb, opposed their relationship. In what might be considered an act of rebellion, at age twenty-five Ada and her boyfriend left their small town of Magrath, Alberta, in Canada in the spring of 1914 to vacation in the big city Calgary. Jack was conceived there. While almost nothing is known about the reaction of Ada's family or the community to her unplanned pregnancy, it can be assumed that in the small, tight-knit, conservative community of Magrath, my grandmother was likely to have been subject to ridicule and shame. Apparently, John Lye Gibb discouraged Ada from marrying the boyfriend, so after Jack was born, Ada and Jack lived with John and his wife Sarah, who showed love and support for both Ada and the baby.

At the same time, George William Dyer lived in Lake Oswego, Oregon. In 1921, "Will"—as he was called—was age forty-nine and single. He worked odd jobs and was an attendant at the boat house on the lake in the town. His mother, Jehzeel, was concerned that Will might never get married and communicated that concern to her half sister, Sarah Gibb (John Lye Gibb's wife). Sarah, on the other hand, had a thirty-two-year-old daughter with a seven-year-old son whose prospects for marriage in Magrath were virtually nil. They arranged for Ada to travel to Oregon to meet Will and see if a marriage could be manufactured. To the sisters' delight, Ada and Will agreed to be married, with Ada having the understanding that Will would adopt Jack and give him the Dyer name. This would hopefully remove the stigma associated with Jack's birth. Ada and Will were married in 1921, but after the wedding Will's mother, Jehzeel, objected to Jack's adoption; to my grandmother's dismay Jack was never adopted and carried the Gibb surname for the rest of his life.

Ada and Will had six children together, two girls and four boys—including my father, William ("Bill") Gibb Dyer. Jack was ten at the time of Bill's birth, and my father recounted that as he was growing up he was never told by his parents who Jack was or what his relationship was to him—he just knew there was an older boy living in his home whose name was Jack Gibb. Ada and Will never discussed how Jack came to be in their home. Eventually, when my father was older, Jack told him how he came to be a part of the Dyer family.

After my grandparents were married they moved to Portland, Oregon where Will opened a small grocery store. Jack and the other children worked in the store. During the summer break from school, Jack would often go back to Magrath to see his grandparents and earn money working on one of the farms in the area. Jack wrote about a letter he received from Will during one summer in Magrath:

I remember receiving a letter from my stepfather when I was

spending the summer working on the farm of a relative. . . .
He asked me to find my real father, who he thought lived
near Magrath, and never to return to his home in Portland,
Oregon. I remember, at the age of fifteen, understanding the
feelings of my stepfather, who deeply resented taking care of
his wife's bastard son. I must have been a continuing reminder
of the "sin" that his wife had committed. I could easily understand his feelings. At the same time I was deeply frightened
and had no way of knowing how to find my own father, who
I had never met and whose name I did not know. I missed
my mother, felt that I had nowhere to turn, and felt friendless
and abandoned and resentful of [Will's] action. I felt caught
between my strong compassion for him and his pain, and my
strong feelings of fear, impotence, and abandonment.[1]

Jack eventually left home to attend college, and after a number
of years of schooling he graduated with a PhD in psychology from
Stanford University. He had a successful career as an academic and
a consultant, but he never got over the feelings of betrayal and abandonment he felt from his birth father and from Will. I believe the
issue of trust was a major factor in Jack's two failed marriages and
his attempt to create utopian societies through what he called "TORI
Communities" (TORI standing for Trust, Openness, Responsibility,
and Insight). His most important book is titled *Trust*, which discusses
his attempt to build trust in his own life and the lives of others.[2]

Chapter 4 discussed the cultural assumption regarding trusting
others, and this chapter will cover trust in depth. I will first discuss
how to define trust and review its origins, and then examine why trust
is lost in families and what can be done to restore it. The latter part
of the chapter will review trends in family structure worldwide that
would tend to undermine trust in families. Finally, the "Family Trust
Survey" will help you see the degree of trust in your family and identify
potential problems.

What Is Trust?

Trust has been defined as "a psychological state comprising the intention to accept vulnerability based on positive expectations of the intentions or behavior of another."[3] In other words, people agree to be vulnerable in some way based on the belief that a relationship to a person, a group, or an institution will be beneficial. Three types of trust are in families:[4]

» *Interpersonal trust*, which is based on one's relationship and history with another person. To the extent that another person has proven to be predictable and behaves reliably in certain situations, the person is deemed to be trustworthy. In Jack Gibb's case, he was unable to build a trusting relationship with his stepfather and his abandonment by his birth father exacerbated his feelings of insecurity.

» *Competence trust*, which is based on the skills, abilities, and experience of the other party. If the other person has the necessary expertise to help with a particular concern or problem, his or her judgment and advice are trusted. A person's status in the family, academic degrees, certifications, reputation, etc. are often the ways people "know" someone can be trusted. We trust that our credentialed doctors know what they are doing.

» *Institutional trust*, which is based on whether the family, the system, the rules, or the processes are seen as being fair and trustworthy. Family members want to know if they will have a place to stay, food to eat, and social support. They also want to know if they can air grievances when not treated fairly in the family and receive a fair hearing.

The Psychological Origins of Trust

The psychologist Erik Erikson's theorizing about the origins of trust can help us to understand why my Uncle Jack would have had difficulty with this issue. Erikson postulated that all of us have a basic dilemma to resolve during childhood—can we trust the world around us or is the world basically unsafe and unworthy of trust?[5] Erikson argues that to develop trust children need to grow up in a predictable world where food, shelter, protection, and affection are a given. But when they grow up in environments plagued by constant change and uncertainty, children come to view the world with fear and suspicion. If a family—in particular, the parents—creates a safe and predictable environment, the children will grow up to trust those around them. That's why single parenthood can create uncertainty for children, given that resources aren't supplied by two parents and that there may be multiple adults (boyfriends or girlfriends) moving in and out of the children's lives. However, a person's beliefs about trust, while primarily formed in early childhood, must also be negotiated throughout life. If, for example, a child has a supportive, trusting home life that is disrupted by a messy divorce during his teenage years, this teenager may doubt the security he once had and begin to see the world as more uncertain and less trustworthy.

People also develop trust as they interact with others. Trust regarding family members tends to be more situation-specific and nuanced. For example, a sister may trust her brother to help her do her homework correctly, but she knows not to trust him in a card game since he's been known to cheat. These "repeated plays" where we have the opportunity to test trustworthiness allow family members to better predict how others in the family will behave in certain situations. And, of course, people tend to want verbal commitments from other parties when unsure of their trustworthiness; with much uncertainty from the other party, people might rely on written or legal documents to ensure proper behavior and which provide recourse.

Why Is Trust So Important?

Research on trust shows that trusting relationships are particularly valuable in families.[6] Trust lowers "transactions costs," or the costs related to contracting with others for help. By trusting family members, legal documents or other costly and time-consuming legal mechanisms are unnecessary to ensure agreements will be kept. Trust also lowers "agency costs" (i.e., costs associated with monitoring others) because those trusted don't need to be monitored. Trust also tends to enhance the self-esteem of family members and can lead to more creative and innovative behaviors, since family members will not feel the need to protect themselves from others. In low-trust families, family members often spend time covering their actions to avoid retribution; communications are often restricted and distorted, and conflict often leads to poor outcomes. Trust matters since it allows individuals to interact in a cooperative and productive manner.

Potential Problems with Family Trust

Trust can prove problematic in certain situations. Anthropologist Edward Banfield, in his classic work *The Moral Basis of a Backward Society*, described problems faced by communities in southern Italy when trust was isolated to members of each person's own family and not extended to outsiders.[7] Important community assets such as schools and roads in southern Italy were not supported, since local families were unwilling to trust and cooperate with one another; Banfield labeled such behavior "amoral familism." Francis Fukuyama, in his book titled *Trust,* writes that "familistic societies frequently have weak voluntary associations because unrelated people have no basis for trusting one another."[8] The importance of social capital that goes beyond a person's nuclear family cannot be overstated since it leads to healthy individuals, families, communities, and economies.[9] Thus there is a "dark side" to trust if it becomes too insular and undermines building trusting relationships and social capital with those outside the family.

The social capital literature describes differences between bonding and bridging social capital.[10] *Bonding social capital* concerns building trust and strong relationships within a group (e.g., the family), whereas *bridging social capital* involves creating strong relationships between the group and those outside the group. Those entrepreneurs or families with Banfield's amoral familism orientation tend to generate strong bonds within the family to the detriment of bridging relationships with those outside the family network.

Consistent with this line of theorizing, Professors Julie Hite and Bill Hesterly summarize some of the constraints entrepreneurs face when they rely too much on their families:

> Several studies show that emerging firms tend to leverage ties with entrepreneurs' family members and friends to gain the key resources needed to establish firm viability. . . . Thus the image is of an entrepreneur drawing resources from a cohesive network of embedded ties . . . [but] cohesive networks are a source of more constraint than advantage for emerging firms.[11]

Hite and Hesterly rightly point out that in attempting to grow a large business it is important to create a broader resource network outside the family so one won't be constrained by possibly limited family resources. And as discussed in chapter 1, the "superstar entrepreneurs" rely less on family capital than other youths and appear to go outside the family for resources.

Even if you are not an entrepreneur, your life can be enhanced and resources gained by building bridges with those outside your family.

How Is Trust Violated?

There appear to be two primary means by which trust is violated:

» Acts of commission—an individual, group, or organization does or says something inconsistent with your expectations. Hence, trust has been violated.

» Acts of omission—someone (or a group or organization) fails to do something expected.

Moreover, apparently not all violations of trust are viewed equally. From my experience as a consultant to many family firms, the following list orders various violations of trust from the most to the least serious:

- » Infidelity.
- » Violations of the law (e.g., stealing, forgery, drug use). Such violations can lead to the filing of formal complaints or lawsuits against other family members.
- » Lying.
- » Failure to meet obligations (financial or otherwise).
- » Failure to follow agreed-upon procedures.
- » Lack of transparency—the lack of sharing or withholding of information from others in the family. Donald Trow discovered in his seminal study of small businesses many years ago that families that shared succession plans with other family members in a demonstration of trust had fewer problems in managing succession, and the firm fared better financially afterward, than those families who did not share succession plans.[12]

How Can Trust Be Repaired?

In my experience, trust is easily lost—we, members of our families, and the organizations we belong to are all fallible, and at times expectations are unfulfilled. Losing trust, unfortunately, is quite easy, while regaining it can be incredibly hard.

Repairing Interpersonal Trust

The following steps are important when repairing interpersonal trust:

1. **Confession.** Does the person admit his or her mistake and ask for forgiveness?
2. **Remorse.** Is the offender really sorry? Sincerity is important for those who want to trust the offender again. Showing true remorse is often essential to receive forgiveness and begin to repair the trust.
3. **Attribution.** Was the violation a result of the situation or some personality flaw? If the person who was harmed by the violation sees the breakdown of trust as

situational—something that was caused by an unusual set of circumstances—trust is more easily repaired than if one believes that the offender has a fundamental character flaw that makes him or her difficult to trust.

4. **Transformation.** Is the problem fixable? Can the person change? If the person harmed believes that someone who violated trust can change, that person would be more willing to begin anew to build trust with that individual. For repeated violations of trust, restoration of trust will be more difficult. That's true even if the offender goes a long period since the last repetition of the offense.

5. **Restitution.** Can the person make up for what was lost due to the violation of trust? If a person has hurt another's reputation, he must act to restore that reputation; if someone has been hurt financially, she needs to be compensated for the loss. To the extent that restitution is difficult, if not impossible (as in cases of infidelity or murder), repairing trust becomes all that more difficult.

6. **Willingness to extend forgiveness.** Even if the offender goes through the steps to repair trust, it will not be restored unless the offended party forgives the offender and again becomes vulnerable to a degree with the offender.

Repairing Competence Trust

Repairing competence trust in a family may involve one or more of the following actions:

» Support schooling or other types of training to improve a family member's skills and abilities.

» Encourage honest, open, and supportive feedback within the family to help family members recognize their weaknesses and develop plans to improve.

» Develop fair and consistent disciplinary procedures to deal with family members who violate expectations in the family and provide support for family members to restore lost trust.

» Require credentials certifying competence. Some families, such as the Haas family at Levi Strauss, required family members to get an MBA degree before being allowed to work in the family business. Other families that I am aware of require significant work experience outside the family business before allowing the family member to work for the family.

Repairing Institutional Trust

Repairing institutional trust—trust in the family—generally requires creating systems and processes that allow for transparency. The following are just some of the activities that help to repair institutional trust:

» Clarify and share the details regarding what will happen when one or both parents die. Sharing your will with your children (when they reach an appropriate age) can build feelings of trust and confidence between parent and child. When I teach classes on succession in family businesses, I ask my students, "Do you know if your parents have a will, and if so, have you seen it?" More than 90 percent of my students don't know if their parents have a will, and only about 10 percent of those who do (or 1 percent of the total) have been given the opportunity to read it and ask questions.

» Share pertinent financial information regarding family assets with family members on a regular basis. In my case, my wife, Theresa, and I meet with our sons and daughters and their spouses once a year to review our will and to discuss our financial condition. We do this to ensure no significant surprises arise for them when we are gone.

» Ensure that the processes for making important decisions are transparent (e.g., activities such as vacations or important purchases that would affect the family).

The Role of Third Parties in Repairing Trust

In the case of violation of interpersonal trust within a family—particularly if it's a serious violation such as infidelity—a family may need a therapist or counselor to restore the relationship. In my role as a family business consultant, I've often been aided by a family therapist. Given that I have neither the training nor credentials for family therapy, attempting to engage in therapy with a client would be unethical. However, given my background and training, it's entirely appropriate for me to work with a client to clarify various simple conflicts and violations of trust or to help the family create a plan of action to repair competence or institutional trust. I generally do so by the following:

» Encouraging the family to set clear guidelines and expectations for family members and outline the consequences for not meeting those expectations.

» Engaging in team building activities that help the family clarify how decisions are made and how the family might work as a team.[13]

» Clarifying the family's mission—helping the family create a mission statement or statement of values as was described in the previous chapter. Ivan Lansberg, in his book *Succeeding Generations*, describes how he works with families to commit to a "shared dream" that they can all support, which creates unity and trust within the family.[14]

» Encouraging family members to get additional schooling and training to help them prepare for their futures and to help the family when needed.

» Encouraging transparency in the sharing of information, decision-making, etc. Family councils provide a means for expressing transparency. A mediator may be needed to help set up the meetings.

Consultants and counselors to families should recognize that trust is often based on whether someone believes she is treated fairly.[15] The definition of "fair" often differs among family members. Some may define it as all family members being equal (e.g., all children should receive the same amount of money in their parents' will). Others may think that fairness should be based on merit (e.g., family members who contribute more should receive greater rewards), while others may believe that fairness should be based on need (e.g., more family resources should go to those family members who need more help). Thus, the role of the consultant is often to clarify what the family members believe is fair and help them come to a consensus so that expectations will not be violated.

Fairness not only involves the criteria we use to make decisions, but it also concerns whether a fair process is used when arriving at a family decision.[16] I have witnessed significant variance in families when decisions are made. In some families, it is fair if the family patriarch or matriarch makes key decisions for the family by themselves. At the other extreme, some families require a unanimous decision on the part of all affected family members. Other families take votes, with the majority prevailing, while other families involve outside facilitators who ensure that all family members have a voice in whatever decision is made. Regardless of the process used, for family harmony to be maintained, the family needs to examine the process it uses to make decisions and determine what is fair for all family members.

The fair process used in decision-making also depends on the type of decision. For example, in creating a will, the father and mother may have the final say in deciding how their assets should be distributed; but for deciding where to spend a family vacation, a family vote where all can voice their preferences may be the best approach. Depending on the stage of a family's development, certain decision-making methods may be appropriate (e.g., when children are young, the parents should probably make the decisions), but as a family evolves, new decision-making approaches often need to be adopted.

Problems of Trust for Families in the Future

When examining the global trends regarding family structure presented earlier in this book, you may ask whether families of the future will likely have more or fewer issues related to trust as they attempt to create and sustain family capital. Several global trends are likely to make developing trust more difficult in the future, including escalating divorce rates and increasing numbers of single-parent families. Divorce naturally undermines trust between parents and children, since it often brings greater uncertainty into children's lives. Additionally, blended families formed after divorce often face trust issues. (See chapter 2 for a more in-depth discussion of divorce and chapter 3 for case studies of turbulent family paths that may follow divorce.)

Children from single-parent families grow up in a more threatening world. (See chapter 2 for a discussion of how single-parent families can contribute to economic, behavioral, educational, and emotional problems.[17]) These findings suggest that societies with a high percentage of single-parent families will have less human capital available to support a family or potentially launch a business as compared to societies with fewer single parents. If this is the case, Asian families will have an advantage in human capital for their societies and their family businesses.

If trust has indeed been declining in families due to disruptions in family structure, an effect will be noticed in businesses outside of family businesses. Those organizations will likely have more challenges because their employees will come from families that lack family capital and are unstable. If today's children develop an inherent distrust of others due to experiences in their families, how will they function in the organizations of the future? Given current trends regarding the family, we'll likely see the following:

- » More employees with emotional and behavioral problems
- » More employees who distrust members of their team or department and are therefore less willing to collaborate

» Fewer employees willing to trust authority figures, particularly their immediate bosses

» Fewer employees willing to engage with and commit to an organization

Both theory and practice in the field of management points to the importance of building trust in organizations to obtain optimal results. Unfortunately, current trends regarding the family suggest that building such trust may be difficult.

Chapter Takeaways

» High levels of trust correlate with good family outcomes.

» Family members can lose interpersonal, competence, and institutional trust, but they can regain it.

» Although repairing trust is difficult, research and practice have suggested approaches for doing so.

» Lack of trust in the general population will likely negatively affect family and nonfamily businesses.

Family Trust Survey

1. To what extent do family members feel that they can be open with one another regarding any concerns?

   Very little extent   *To a great extent*

   1   2   3   4   5

2. To what extent are family members willing to give negative feedback to other family members?

   Very little extent   *To a great extent*

   1   2   3   4   5

3. To what extent do family members feel they can contribute in family decision-making?

   Very little extent   *To a great extent*

   1   2   3   4   5

4. To what extent do family members feel they could loan money to other family members and be repaid?

   Very little extent   *To a great extent*

   1   2   3   4   5

5. To what extent do family members avoid blaming one another for their problems?

   Very little extent   *To a great extent*

   1   2   3   4   5

6. To what extent do family members avoid being critical of other family members behind their backs?

   Very little extent   *To a great extent*

   1   2   3   4   5

7. To what extent do family members share sensitive information about themselves with other family members?

   Very little extent   *To a great extent*

   1   2   3   4   5

8. To what extent are family members willing to share their resources with other family members?
Very little extent   *To a great extent*
1   2   3   4   5

9. To what extent do you feel that family members are competent and have important skills?
Very little extent   *To a great extent*
1   2   3   4   5

10. To what extent are adult children in your immediate family aware of what should happen with their parents' assets should they die or be incapacitated?
Very little extent   *To a great extent*
1   2   3   4   5

11. In the past, to what extent have family members avoided violating trust in the family?
Very little extent   *To a great extent*
1   2   3   4   5

12. To what extent do family members feel secure in their relationships with one another?
Very little extent   *To a great extent*
1   2   3   4   5

Scoring: Total up your score, ranging from 12 to 60. Scores from 48 to 60 would indicate high trust in the family. Scores from 36 to 47 would indicate moderate trust, and scores below 36 would indicate that significant trust issues exist in the family.

Notes

1. Jack R. Gibb, "The Passionate Path," 1983, http://www.oocities.org/toritrust/passionate_
   path.htm.
2. Jack R. Gibb, *Trust* (North Hollywood, CA: Newcastle Publishing, 1978).
3. Peter H. Kim, Kurt T. Dirks, and Cecily D. Cooper, "The Repair of Trust: A Dynamic
   Bilateral Perspective and Multilevel Conceptualization," *Academy of Management Review*
   34 no. 3 (2009): 401.
4. Chamu Sundaramurthy, "Sustaining Trust Within Family Businesses," *Family Business
   Review* 21 no. 1 (2008): 89–102.
5. Erik H. Erikson, *Identity and the Life Cycle* (New York: W. W. Norton, 1994).
6. William S. Schulze et al., "Agency Relationships in Family Firms: Theory and Evidence,"
   Organization Science 12 no. 2 (2001): 99–116.
7. Edward C. Banfield, *The Moral Basis of a Backward Society* (Glencoe, IL: The Free Press,
   1958).
8. Francis Fukuyama, *Trust: The Social Virtues and the Creation of Prosperity* (New York: Free
   Press, 1996): 28–29.
9. Robert D. Putnam, *Bowling Alone: The Collapse and Revival of American Community* (New
   York: Simon and Schuster, 1999).
10. Paul S. Adler and Seok Woo Kwon, "Social Capital: Prospects for a New Concept,"
    Academy of Management Review 27 no. 1 (2002): 17–40.
11. Julie M. Hite and William S. Hesterly, "The Evolution of Firm Networks: From Emergence
    to Early Growth of the Firm," *Strategic Management Journal* 22 (2001): 275–76.
12. Donald B. Trow, "Executive Succession in Small Companies," *Administrative Science
    Quarterly* 6 no. 2 (1961): 228–39.
13. Gibb Dyer and Jeff Dyer, *Beyond Team Building* (New York: Wiley, 2019).
14. Ivan Lansberg, *Succeeding Generations* (Boston: Harvard Business School Press, 1999).
15. Ludo Van der Heyden, Christine Blondel, and Randel S. Carlock, "Fair Process: Striving for
    Justice in Family Business," *Family Business Review* 18 no. 1 (2005): 1–21.
16. Ibid.
17. See also, Sara McLanahan, "Fragile Families and the Reproduction of Poverty," *Annals of
    the American Academy of Political and Social Science* 621 no. 1 (2009): 111–31.

I had a really wonderful upbringing. We were a tight family. It was wonderful to grow up with so many siblings. . . . I learned everything from my older brother and sister and taught it to my younger sisters.

Joaquin Phoenix, actor

CHAPTER 7

HOW DO WE TRANSFER FAMILY CAPITAL TO THE NEXT GENERATION?

As a doctoral student at MIT in the early 1980s, I was the teaching assistant to Professor Dick Beckhard, a well-known business consultant and a friend of my father (again the advantage of family social capital). One day, when I was eating lunch with Dick, he asked, "Gibb, what do you know about family businesses?" I admitted that I didn't know much about them, only that my grandfather ran a family-owned grocery store in Portland, Oregon, for many years and that my great-grandfather operated a family business with his sons in Alberta, Canada. Dick explained that many of his clients owned family businesses and were extremely difficult to work with. He would try to help his clients solve various business issues only to have family conflicts and dynamics undermine his consulting work. He then proposed that we invite some of his clients to Boston, listen to their problems, and develop a research agenda based on family business issues. When Dick's family business clients arrived, I spent three days learning about situations I never encountered in my MBA program, which had focused primarily on challenges facing large, public corporations. Although the clients discussed family conflicts, nepotism, the role of nonfamily managers in family firms, and such, the issue that most concerned them was *succession* in the family business—the transfer of ownership, management, and values from one generation to the next. Since that time, I have researched and consulted about the succession problem. Transferring family capital to the next generation poses difficulties most families do not handle well; conflicts between and within generations can lead to poor outcomes. Poor estate planning often results in paying too many taxes or leaving wealth to the wrong people; a lack of planning for the transfer of family capital across generations can lead to a loss of that capital, leaving future generations deficient.

Given these challenges, in this chapter I will discuss problems related to the issue and outline a process I believe can help. A checklist at the end of the chapter will help you determine your family's situation.

Why Families Don't Plan to Transfer Family Capital

For some families, the transfer of family capital to the next generation proceeds naturally. Because of the culture, family elders teach their children or other younger family members what they need to know to succeed in life and imbue them with values they believe will be helpful. Moreover, the family leaders look for opportunities to provide experiences for younger family members whether through full- or part-time employment, internships, traveling to gain experience, or working on projects together. Family leaders often foot the bill or give their time for these experiences, making it easier for the younger family members to participate. Certain wealthy families also provide support to future generations through trusts or other mechanisms that provide financial resources to help family members launch successful careers.

Unfortunately, in my experience, families that successfully transfer family capital to the next generation are in the minority. Evidence of the lack of planning for transferring family capital can be seen in the number of people that have created a will—the primary mechanism to transfer financial wealth to the next generation. According to a recent survey, 51 percent of Americans age fifty-five to sixty-four do not have a will (moreover, 68 percent of African American adults and 74 percent of Hispanic adults in that age group have not drafted that important document).[1] Although some families have wills to transfer family financial capital, I find that even fewer have plans to transfer family human and social capital to the next generation. Those types of capital can be even more valuable than tangible resources.

Several reasons explain why family elders fail to plan for the transfer of family capital, including the following more common ones.

Fear of Death

A number of clients have told me they think the act of creating a will or doing succession planning is akin to "planning my own funeral." Most of us do not want to think about death. One of the family leaders that I met in the Boston meetings gave the following analogy to illustrate the depth of his feelings about succession planning:

> Succession planning . . . is really digging your own grave. It's preparing for your own death and it's very difficult to make contact with the concept of death emotionally. . . . It is a kind of *seppuku*—the *hara-kiri* that Japanese commit. [It's like] putting a dagger to your belly . . . and having someone behind you cut off your head. . . . That analogy sounds dramatic, but emotionally it's close to it. You're ripping yourself apart—your power, your significance, your leadership, your father role.[2]

While not all of us have such deep, negative feelings regarding planning for a future where we are not in the picture, such feelings are common and can prevent creating a plan to transfer family capital to the next generation.

Fear of Loss of Power and Status

One common characteristic of family firm owners that I have worked with is the tendency to be secretive and avoid sharing resources with others. The knowledge, contacts, and financial resources held by family leaders gives them the power and status that they need (and sometimes crave) to influence others and get things done. Giving that up by sharing information, contacts, or other resources can cause much discomfort. Family elders may want to always have a "one up" on others in the family, particularly their children or others in the next generation, so there is little incentive to share with them.

The Need to Feel Useful

All of us want to be seen as a valuable contributor to our families and to society. Unfortunately, some see retirement and handing over the reins of leadership to the next generation as diminishing their sense of worth and value to the family and to society. One family business leader said the following:

> I could [not] care less about retiring. The guys that I know that are successful and do well are the ones who never retire. . . . A good way of dying fast is going from being busy to doing nothing. I don't think I'll ever stop working. . . . I'd rather have something to do to keep me busy. Otherwise, I'd go nuts. You can't just get in a rocking chair and waste your life away.[3]

If family elders see the transferring of family capital to the next generation as diminishing their usefulness and role in the family, they are less likely to do so.

Lack of Trust in the Next Generation

I have found numerous family leaders who are reluctant to transfer their family capital due to lack of confidence in their progeny. Some see an entitlement mentality in the next generation and believe their heirs to be irresponsible and likely to squander the resources. Their concern is not unreasonable, since several studies of family businesses have found that second and third generations are often poor stewards of family resources—and as a result the family firm does poorly or goes bankrupt.⁴ One study by the Williams Group reported that 70 percent of wealthy families lose their wealth by the second generation and 90 percent by the third.⁵ The survey further noted that 78 percent of the respondents didn't think that the next generation was prepared for an inheritance, and therefore 64 percent had shared little or no information about the status of their wealth with their heirs.⁶ Some wealth advisors have been overheard saying, "The first generation makes it, the second spends it, and the third blows it." Thus, if there is little trust in the next generation, there is little incentive to plan for the transfer of family capital.

Lack of Knowledge

Many do not understand how to transfer capital or even that they need a plan. Whereas informal sharing in the home happens spontaneously, transferring *key* knowledge and skills often happens only with planning—particularly if a family wants to maintain social relations with those who can help them. Maintaining strong social ties to important people across generations should not be left to chance. Yet I find that many family businesses flounder after a leader is incapacitated or dies suddenly, because he has not helped the next generation join the social network.

What Can Happen with No Preparation

When family leaders fail to transfer family capital, the outcomes can be devastating. One wealthy business owner died unexpectedly without preparing for the transfer of important knowledge and social contacts. His son reflected on what a severe blow it was to him and his family:

> On the day of my father's funeral, the family had to go to his office and break into the locked bottom right drawer of his desk. He always said if something happened to him, that was

where the important stuff was. You don't know how many
times I later sat at that same desk crying, wishing my father
had spent an hour with me explaining what it all meant. The
professional advisors tried to be helpful, but I just didn't understand the relationships. . . . Sure, I had worked in the firm for
a couple of summers doing office stuff, but it was primarily
secretarial and I really didn't pay much attention to how the
business was really run, who the key players were. I could have
learned more. People could have taught me more. . . . We simply weren't prepared for his passing—on the home front or the
business front.[7]

Unfortunately, this situation is all too common.

Sometimes family capital is transferred, but younger family
members are unprepared to handle the responsibility—particularly
financial capital. One successful founder confided in me that she felt
her children weren't prepared and were ill-served when she had to sell
her company unexpectedly. Her children had received gifts of company stock, making them instant millionaires. She explained:

The number one change that we would make today, had we
known that we were going to sell the company, would be to
not give our children 49 percent of our business in stock.
Our children would first have to earn their own money, get
an education, go into careers of their own choice, buy their
first homes, struggle to buy their furniture, have direction,
and accomplish goals. To actually know the thrill of what it
is to achieve success on their own. We feel that this is an area
that we as their parents totally lost control of and that we have
done a big disservice to our children. And it is a big concern
to us. Of course, they would be shocked at hearing me say this.
They are thrilled to have this wonderful opportunity to have
new houses, to go golfing every day, to be able to do whatever
they want. But they received too much money too soon, and
it could really be a curse to them in the future. . . . They will
never know or understand the true value of achievement.[8]

How to Encourage Family Leaders to Transfer Family Capital

One of my most significant challenges has been to motivate family leaders to transfer family capital. The noted psychologist Erik Erikson describes *generativity*, his term for that which motivates individuals to be concerned about the well-being and success of the next generation.[9] Erikson believes that most people have a concern about leaving a legacy—the need to leave their mark on the world—which emerges toward later stages in life. People generally see that they can preserve their legacy through their children or other family members. Generativity can impel them to begin transferring family capital to their heirs.

Nevertheless, my clients are often not motivated until a health crisis or dangerous experience causes them to face death. I have always wished for some ethical way to give my clients a near-death experience to encourage them to change. Unfortunately, I haven't figured out how to do that yet.

A more practical approach that I have used is to get them involved in organizations such as the Young Presidents Organization and their local chamber of commerce, where they can meet people like themselves who have faced or are facing the challenge of passing on their wealth. Listening to stories of success and failure from others in a similar situation tends to help my clients see the value of preparing their descendants for a future without them. I also share with them the sad statistics regarding the performance of the business and the health of the family when family leaders don't prepare the next generation of leaders.[10] Despite my best efforts, I still experience failures in helping family leaders develop and carry out a succession plan.

How to Transfer Family Capital

Transferring family capital requires the family to answer the following questions:

» What kinds of family capital (human, social, financial) will be helpful to future generations?
» What family capital do we currently have that needs to be transferred?
» Who has access to this family capital? Or, if we don't have the needed family capital, how do we develop it for future generations?

If family leaders don't start the process, younger family members may need to bring these issues to the attention of their elders, since months or years may be needed for the transfer of family capital. Raising these issues is not easy, because the elders may view the younger generation unfavorably. No one wants to be seen as a gold-digger or as someone who wants to hasten a parent's demise. This is when high levels of trust—discussed in the previous chapter—should smooth the process.

To facilitate the process of transferring knowledge, skills, and social contacts, doing the following is useful:

1. Create a genogram of one's nuclear and extended family.
2. Create a family capital genogram that identifies who has access to family capital.
3. Develop a plan to improve relationships between those who have family capital and those who need it.
4. Develop specific plans to transfer family capital from one person to another by using the "learning by doing" approach, which sometimes requires getting outside help (e.g., lawyers, accountants).

Creating a Family Genogram

Family genograms are a diagnostic tool to help families understand how their family functions.[11] Figure 7.1 is a genogram of the hypothetical Williams family. I have listed four generations, although in most cases three is sufficient. In figure 7.2 are listed the various symbols found in the genogram and what they mean.

In figure 7.1 the squares designate men and the circles designate women. An "x" through either a square or circle denotes that the person has died. For the Williams family, all of the individuals listed in the first generation have passed away. In the second generation, Ryan and Annie are married and have a "typical" relationship—neither close nor distant. Ryan had a close relationship (two lines between people) with his Uncle Sam, while Annie had close relationships with her father and mother, though the latter was fraught with conflict (as noted by the lightning symbol). Ryan has a close relationship with his daughter Holly but has had significant conflicts with his two sons, Mitch and Drew. Annie has distant relationships with Holly and Drew (as noted by a dashed line) but a close relationship with her son Mitch. In the third generation, Eric and Holly—who are married—have a "fused" relationship (three lines between them), meaning that one generally doesn't do anything without the other's input and consent. Moreover, Eric and Holly have a close relationship with their children Ashley and Ben, who have a close sibling relationship with one another. Mitch and Missy, on the other hand, are divorced (noted by two diagonal lines between them). As a result, Mitch's son, Tim, has cut off their relationship (noted by one diagonal line between them)— they haven't communicated with each other in several years. However, Missy—Tim's mother—has a close relationship with him (Missy had sole custody of Tim after the divorce). Drew and Katy are in a close, cohabiting relationship (a dotted line like those who are married) and have two sons together. Drew has a close relationship to Evan but a distant relationship with Jake, while Katy has just the opposite relationships with the boys—close to Jake but distant from Evan. Jake and Evan have a distant relationship.

Though not depicted in the Williams genogram, families whose members have serious physical or mental challenges should denote that by shading the left side of the appropriate circle or square, while families whose members have substance abuse challenges should denote that by shading the bottom part of the related figure. Because such individuals often need significant family resources to help them with their challenges, they should be represented.

Figure 7.1 Williams Family Genogram

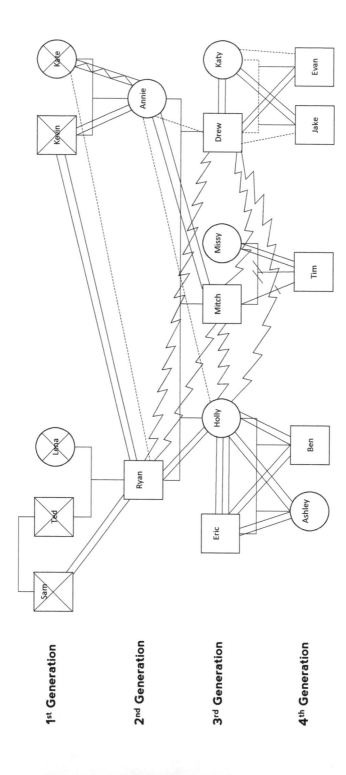

Figure 7.2 Reading a Genogram

Males are drawn as squares, females as circles   Male = ☐   Female = ○

Name (and possibly age) is shown within
the square or the circle. Death is indicated
by an X through the symbol.

Couples are shown by a line connecting their
symbols as follows:

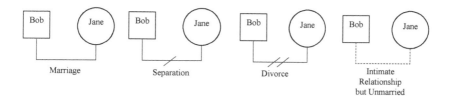

In addition to lines showing kindship, a second set of
lines can show emotional relationships as follows:

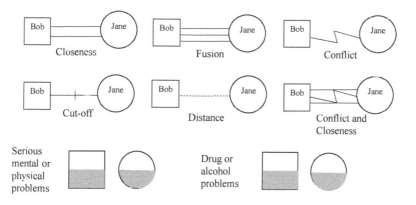

Develop the Family Capital Genogram

Because family capital is generally not transferred when the relationship is conflicted or missing, a genogram provides insight relevant to the transfer. Once the initial genogram is created, a family capital genogram can be constructed (see figure 7.3). To do so, one determines the human, social, and financial capital held by each person. In figure 7.3, human capital is designated by "HC," social capital by "SC," and financial capital by "FC." One asterisk (*) designates modest family capital on that dimension, two asterisks (**) medium capital, and three asterisks (***) means that the person is high on that particular dimension. If HC, SC, or FC are not listed next to a person's name, that indicates no significant family capital along that dimension. Those creating the family capital genogram should develop a list for each person that specifies the relevant human, social, and financial capital. For example, if Holly has a particular social network, the people in that network should be identified along with what could potentially be gleaned from each; or if Annie is known to have $2 million in liquid assets, that should be listed.

In the case of the Williams family, Ryan's Uncle Sam has a rich social network, even though he is dead. But that network can still be valuable. In my case, I can call on friends of my father to provide advice and help even though he has been gone for more than twenty years. In the Williams family, Ryan is the conduit through which Sam's relationships flow; for someone in the Williams family to connect with this social network they would typically need to have a good relationship with Ryan. Thus Holly—Ryan's daughter—might gain access to Sam's social network, whereas Mitch and Drew would likely need to repair their relationship with their father to gain access (although a family member could perhaps go around someone in the family to

Family Capital Designations

HC—Human Capital	*Low
SC—Social Capital	**Medium
FC—Financial Capital	***High

No * indicates little or no family capital.

Figure 7.3 Williams Family Capital Genogram

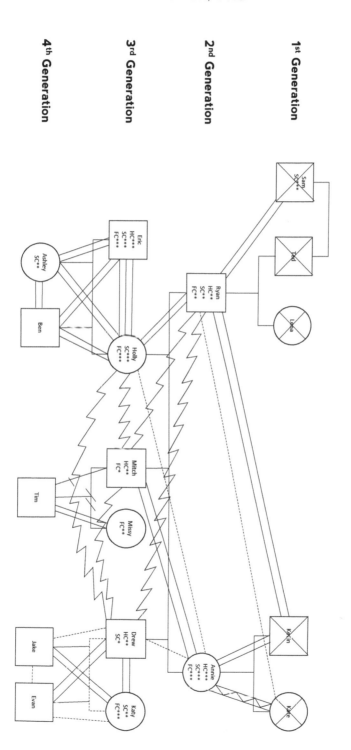

1st Generation

2nd Generation

3rd Generation

4th Generation

access his or her network). Figure 7.3 also shows that Annie had close relationships with her parents, but neither one has significant family capital. However, Annie has significant human, social, and financial capital. Because of Mitch's close relationship with his mother, Annie, he is likely to be able to draw upon her rich resource network, whereas Holly and Drew probably won't be able to influence their mother to help them if a need were to arise. Eric and Holly's family members would likely share family capital with one another, since they have close relationships and could help one another; both Eric and Holly have significant family capital and their daughter Ashley has access to social capital. Tim likely won't be able to go to his father, Mitch, for help, but his mother Missy's social network is available to him. Due to Drew's conflicted relationship with his father, Ryan, and a distant relationship with his mother, Annie, he will likely not be able to draw upon resources from either. However, his partner, Katy, has important social and financial capital that could be useful to him. Jake could tap into Katy's resource network while Evan could tap into Drew's resource network, particularly along the dimension of human capital.

Develop Stronger Relationships

After creating the family capital genogram the next step is to strengthen relationships between those in the family who have family capital and those who need it. Building trust between family members is the key to creating stronger family relationships. See chapter 6 for how to repair breakdowns in interpersonal trust, how to develop competence trust, and how to build institutional trust through being more transparent. In the Williams family the cut-off relationship between Mitch and Tim would likely not be repaired without therapy.

Learning by Doing: The Key to Successful Transfer of Family Capital

Over my career as a consultant and educator, I have learned that merely providing my clients and students with information can only get them so far. It's the application of that knowledge in the real world that leads to real learning and positive results. One principle I have learned in helping families transfer family capital is to *make them earn it*! Family capital should not just be given to a person—even though it is relatively easy to transfer money versus transferring social contacts or skills. The recipients of the family capital need to engage in learning that allows them to intimately understand the nature of what they receive.

I have found the "learning by doing" approach to be the most successful method to transfer family capital. The person transferring the family capital would need to identify the type of family capital and potential learning experiences that will help the person acquire and use the family capital effectively. Typically, the person transferring the family capital will mentor the recipients during the process.

J. Willard "Bill" Marriott, founder of the Marriott Corporation, and his parents, Will and Ellen, exemplify my point. At age fourteen, Bill was asked by his father to take a herd of sheep from Ogden, Utah, to San Francisco, California, by train (a distance of about 800 miles); sell them; see the world's fair that was being held there; and then return safely. Bill Marriott's biographer, Robert O'Brien, tells the story about this event:

A moment that he had never even dreamed of arrived in March of 1915. It had been a good winter for the farm, and Will and the lad were playing checkers one evening in the sitting room after supper.

Will, now about fifty, bent his huge frame over the board and pondered his next move. Ellen sat in a rocking chair reading the newspaper by the light of a kerosene lamp on the table beside her chair. There was a hint of spring in the air, and through the screened and open window drifted the cries of the other youngsters and their friends playing hide-and-seek in the valley dusk.

"Son," Will said, "there's something mighty big going on out in California. Have you heard anything about it?"

Bill thought he knew what his father meant, but he hesitated.

Ellen lowered her paper. "Course he has, haven't you, Bill?

There's a story about it right here in the *Standard*."

"I reckon I know what you're talking about," the boy said. "They're having a big world's fair out there in San Francisco."

Will made his move, then leaned back in his chair. "That's right." He studied his son for a moment. "How'd you like to go out there for a few days—see the fair and what some of the rest of the world looks like?"

Bill sat stunned. Sure, he'd been to Star Valley in the Buick and to Salt Lake City, and down to Provo once or twice—but San Francisco, where the trains went? The Pacific Ocean?

He swallowed hard. "Who—me?"

Ellen swung her paper aside. "Not if I have anything to say about it."

"That's right," Will said. "What I've been thinking is this. We've had a good spring with the sheep—two or close to three thousand of them ready for market. Now, out there in 'Frisco, they're running a big exposition all summer long to celebrate the opening of the Panama Canal. There'll be thousands of visitors every day. The restaurants will be needing lots of meat and vegetables and supplies, maybe double what they usually buy. Our lambs will bring a good price, better than Salt Lake or even in Omaha."

The boy couldn't believe it. "And you—you want me to take them there—on a train?"

"Nothing to it," Will said. "We'll herd them up to Ogden, drive them onto the cattle cars, close the gates, and hook 'em up to a train going to 'Frisco."

Bill still couldn't believe it. "Where—where will I ride?"

His father laughed. "Where will you ride? In the caboose, with the crew. You'll be right up there where those little windows are, looking out over the countryside as you go by and learning something about this land of ours."

Ellen shook her head. "Will, that's downright irresponsible. It's putting much too big a load on the boy's shoulders—sending him off nearly a thousand miles to a strange city with thousands of sheep, when he's never been away from home before. What if he gets lost, or gets hurt—?"

The boy looked down at the board. His heart was pounding, and he never forgot what his father did next. The older man stood up, picked up his chair, and carried it over to Ellen's rocker. He sat down and took Ellen's small, work-worn hands in his big ones and looked into her eyes. "Ellen," he said, "Bill's not a boy anymore. He's a young man. For the past few years now, I've been busy with the church and with politics and everything. Maybe there's a lot of things I should have done that I didn't do. But young Bill's stood in for me and taken my place, just like a grown man. He's taken care of the barns and the beets. He's raised lettuce and made us a lot of money. He's taken care of the other children and you, while I've been away. He's ridden herd. Why, he's even shot a couple of bears. What other youngster in the whole valley has done that?"

He looked over at the boy with trust and confidence. "This'll be like rolling off a log for Bill. All we have to do is put those sheep on the cattle cars, and they're locked up. A couple of days on the road, and he's there. And all he has to do on the way is see that those sheep don't fall all over themselves when the train comes to a stop for water or pulls off on a siding to let the express trains pass. I'll give him a long prod pole to take with him, so he can poke 'em up off the floor. That's all there is to it. Ellen, I'd trust him with my life and so would you. Sure as anything, we can trust him with a flock of sheep."[12]

In today's world many parents wouldn't trust their fourteen-year-old son to pick up a gallon of milk at the local grocery store and bring it home, let alone have him take several thousand sheep by train hundreds of miles from home—and with no cell phone to check in! But Will knew that his son needed experience outside of their small farming community and needed the skills related to shipping and selling sheep in order to eventually become an effective farmer. Will had developed an implicit trust in his son—whatever Bill was tasked to do, he did. By the age of fourteen, Bill had already learned how to run the farm, raise crops, help with his siblings, and even shoot a bear—so he had already developed a strong skill set needed on the farm and had developed a sense of self-reliance. And in addition to building the human capital skills of shipping and selling sheep, through this experience Bill would begin to develop a social network. He would interact with people who could help him ship a herd of sheep and—more important—develop relationships with key customers. Thus, it's not particularly surprising that with the business and entrepreneurial skills that Bill learned from his father while growing up on the farm, he was able to launch one of the most successful hotel chains in the world, and help his own children gain the skills they needed to grow the business after he retired.

A variety of approaches are used by families to help transfer family capital using this learning-by-doing approach. For instance, I've seen some family leaders identify formal training—apprenticeships, technical programs, or college degrees—that will help the next generation develop the skills and experience they will need. Family leaders may also work with the next generation on projects or in a business to mentor them. For example, before transferring money to the next generation, a family leader might require the son or daughter to find a job, earn money, and make and keep a budget for a period to demonstrate responsible use of finances. To facilitate this learning, the family leader then provides support for younger family members by helping them in their job searches and teaching them how to manage money and live on a budget.

Recall my previous discussion about how Jon Huntsman took his son Peter (future CEO of Huntsman Chemical) on business trips to help Peter understand how the business worked and to build relationships with key company employees. More importantly, Peter started near the bottom of the organization as an oil truck driver. This allowed Peter to understand the business from the bottom up; demonstrate his competence at various levels in the company; and—most important—begin to develop a social network that, when coupled with his father's social network, would help him in his future role as CEO.

In most instances, outside help will be needed to manage the transfer of family financial capital. Lawyers, accountants, or both will need to draw up a will and determine the tax consequences of transferring assets between generations. In my family, when the children were younger Theresa and I stipulated that, were we both to die, our children could not access their inheritances until age twenty-five. In our absence, my brother David—and later my oldest daughter Emily— were designated as executors of our will to help protect and manage the assets of those children under age twenty-five. Since all my children have now passed that age, any inheritance will flow directly to them when Theresa and I pass away.

Chapter Takeaways

> » Family leaders are sometimes reluctant to pass their knowledge, skills, and contacts to their heirs.
> » For those who take the step, they can create family genograms to smooth the process.
> » The learning-by-doing approach is the most effective way to transfer family capital.

Family Capital Transfer Checklist

1. Do you have a will that designates who will receive your assets when you pass away?
   Yes   No
2. Do you have a living will that outlines your end-of-life wishes?
   Yes   No
3. Do you have a contingency plan to have your assets managed or transferred if you were to die suddenly or be incapacitated for some reason?
   Yes   No
4. Have you identified the human capital you need to transfer to your family members for them to succeed in the future?
   Yes   No
5. Have you identified the social capital you need to transfer to your family members for them to succeed in the future?
   Yes   No
6. Have you identified the financial capital and other tangible assets that you need to transfer to your family members for them to succeed in the future?
   Yes   No
7. Have you identified who needs to receive the various types of family capital?
   Yes   No
8. Do you have a plan to transfer family capital to those family members who will need it?
   Yes   No
9. Does the plan use the "learning-by-doing" approach described in this chapter?
   Yes   No

10. Do you believe you will be successful in transferring family capital to the next generation?
    Yes   No
11. Will your legacy be preserved through your plan of transferring family capital?
    Yes   No
12. Are family members aware of and support your plan to transfer family capital?
    Yes   No

Scoring: If you answered 9–12 "yes" answers, this indicates that you are well on your way to transferring family capital successfully. If you answered 6–8 "yes" answers, this indicates that you are off to a good start. Fewer than 6 "yes" answers indicates that your family is at risk of losing family capital in the future.

Notes

1. "Make A Will Month," *Rocket Lawyer*, 2014, https://www.rocketlawyer.com/news./article-make-a-Will-Month-2014.aspx.

2. Jeffrey H. Dyer, *The Entrepreneurial Experience: Confronting Career Dilemmas of the Start-Up Executive* (San Francisco: Jossey-Bass, 1992), 172.

3. Ibid., 171.

4. Belen Villalonga and Raphael Amit, "How Do Family Ownership, Control, and Management Affect Firm Value?" *Journal of Financial Economics* 80 no. 2 (2006): 385–417.

5. Chris Taylor, "Your Money—A Little Honesty Might Preserve the Family Fortune," *Reuters*, June 17, 2015.

6. Ibid.

7. Lloyd Steier, "Next-Generation Entrepreneurs and Succession: An Exploratory Study of Modes and Means of Managing Social Capital," *Family Business Review* 14 no. 3 (2001): 259–76.

8. Dyer, *The Entrepreneurial Experience: Confronting Career Dilemmas of the Start-Up Executive*, 199–200.

9. Erik H. Erikson, *Identity and the Life Cycle* (New York: W. W. Norton, 1980).

10. Donald B. Trow, "Executive Succession in Small Companies," *Administrative Science Quarterly* 6 no. 2 (1961): 228–39.

11. Jane Hilburt-Davis and William G. Dyer, *Consulting to Family Businesses: Contracting, Assessment, and Implementation* (San Francisco: Jossey-Bass/Pfeiffer, 2003).

12. Robert O'Brien, *Marriott* (Salt Lake City, UT: Deseret Book, 1987), 60–63.

The family is one of nature's
masterpieces.

George Santayana, philosopher

CHAPTER 8

CAN CHURCHES, SCHOOLS, NGOS, AND GOVERNMENT SUBSTITUTE FOR FAMILY CAPITAL?

C an institutions other than the family provide human, social, and financial capital and other important resources to those who need them? In this chapter, I will look specifically at how churches, schools, nongovernmental organizations (NGOs), and governments attempt to provide individuals and families with resources—particularly when they are disadvantaged. If institutions besides the family can provide all key resources, then family capital may be unnecessary or redundant.

To examine this issue we will first look at the functions that families have traditionally filled for their members and then explore how other organizations have increasingly attempted to perform many of those same functions, given that many families are in crisis and unable to meet even the basic needs of family members. I will also critique how well other institutions have performed and look at unintended consequences of aid from these institutions. However, I recognize that I'm only providing a general overview of each institution and its impact. Furthermore, I will focus primarily on what I see happening in the United States.

Changes in Family Functions over Time

Historically, the family has filled most of the functions needed for family members to survive and thrive and, indeed, most family members have expected their families to fulfill these functions.[1] Common functions ascribed to families include providing food, shelter, money, social and emotional support, help in acquiring a mate, education and socialization to cultural norms, and status in society. Before the latter part of the nineteenth and into the twentieth century, families were expected to fulfill most if not all of these functions. However, as families have become more fragile and fragmented, government and other institutions have started to assume some of the burden of these functions. Until the twentieth century, families were almost exclusively responsible for child-care, education, and the care of the elderly. However, by the end of the twentieth century governments and other institutions had largely taken on the particulars of these roles, causing individuals to become more dependent on their institutions rather than their family. In her book *How The West Really Lost God*, Mary Eberstadt observes the current state:

> More people now expect their governments to perform tasks once assumed by sons, daughters, maiden aunts, and the like. As families have shrunk, disbanded, re-formed, and otherwise come to reflect the reality that what were once permanent ties

are now increasingly optional and fungible, Western men and women have ratcheted up the pressure on the state to operate as a family substitute—in particular, as a father substitute. This point was demonstrated perfectly if once more unwittingly in the United States in 2012, when a video made by President Barack Obama's reelection team chronicled a fictitious young woman named "Julia" benefiting from government assistance at each major stage of her life—every one of which forms of assistance, from day care to retirement, are government substitutes for what the extended family was once competent to do and often is no more.[2]

The Role of the Church in Supporting Families

Since the beginning of recorded history, religious movements and churches have helped support individuals and families. They have given people religious and at times secular educational experiences; have provided their members with social capital by facilitating relationships between parishioners; have consoled followers in times of worry and crisis; and have even provided food, shelter, and other necessities for their members. Some sects go so far as to become family-like and fulfill almost all their members' needs. These types of religious groups are often seen by outsiders as "cults," such as the polygamous communities in the American Southwest. Other religions, such as Buddhism, tend to focus more on religious philosophy and play less of an active role in the lives of their adherents.

The following, shared by a clergyman, compellingly shows how churches provide support for their members when family resources are not available:

> I received a phone call from a member of my congregation who informed me that a single mother that he visited had a broken water heater; she had just recently moved from

another state, had no one to help her fix the water heater, and had no money to pay a repairman. She was taking her three children to the local public swimming pool each morning where she and her children could have warm showers. I was shocked that a member of my congregation would be living in such circumstances so I called a plumber who was a church member and asked him if he would fix her water heater for just the cost of the parts. He agreed, and I decided that the church could pay for the parts. I called this woman and told her that I'd heard about her plight and had a solution—her water heater was quickly repaired.

This single mother had no family whom she could call upon for help, so the church stepped in to fill this need. The clergyman also noted that funds from his church are often used to assist with church members' medical and dental expenses, housing costs, utility bills, and such. This support is generally temporary (for a few months at most), as the clergymen work with those receiving support to explore whether extended family can provide needed resources and to develop a plan to help the members become self-reliant.

Of course, churches don't always have the resources needed to remedy a deficit in family capital, and sometimes churches have exploited, rather than supported, their members. But extensive research has shown the impact of religious devotion and church affiliation on individuals and families. In general, the findings suggest that religious observance—defined as regularly attending church, praying, and reading from the faith's scriptures—has the following benefits, irrespective of one's religious preference:[3]

> » Higher levels of marital happiness and stability compared to those without religious ties.
> » Lower levels of divorce: Religious couples are 2.4 times less likely to divorce than nonreligious couples.
> » Stronger parent–child relationships: Religious parents tend to show more affection to children.

» Greater longevity and physical health: Religious persons, on average, live seven years longer than nonreligious persons.
» Higher levels of feelings of well-being.

Moreover, research has shown the following benefits for religious teenagers compared to nonreligious teenagers:

» They are happier and feel more loved compared to those teenagers who aren't religious.
» They have better relationships with their parents, especially the mother.
» They get better grades and are less likely to cheat.
» They are less likely to drink alcohol, smoke, or take drugs.
» They watch less television and play fewer video games.
» They are less sexually active.
» They are more willing to help others.

While religious observance doesn't guarantee a better life, these findings do suggest that being connected to a religious community can provide human, social, and financial capital that greatly stabilizes and helps individuals cope with life's challenges. Churches can also help individuals develop values that will help shape their character. In particular, the religious values that encourage people to delay instant gratification for long-term goals, discourage antisocial behaviors such as crime and drug abuse, and encourage service and helping others tend to lead people to have more productive—and happier—lives. Moreover, the social network gained from church affiliation and the emotional and, at times, financial support from one's religious community are also reasons for the benefits just described.

For churches to provide their members with the advantages of human, social, and financial capital, they need to have people actively involved in the church and its faith community. However, religious affiliation has decreased significantly across the world over the past few decades, particularly in Europe.[4] The Pew Research Center has documented the steady decline of religiosity in the United States. The findings of a survey released in 2015 noted that 67 percent of those individuals born between 1928 and 1945 said that "religion was important in their lives" while only 38 percent of "younger millennials" who were born between 1990 and 1996 reported the same.[5] Therefore, church attendance is declining among most of the major religions in the world.

Several years ago a comprehensive study of America's youth and their orientation toward religion was conducted by Christian Smith, a sociologist at Notre Dame University, with the findings published in his book *Soul Searching: The Religious and Spiritual Lives of American Teenagers*.[6] According to Smith, about 84 percent of the youth thirteen to seventeen years old in the United States are nominally a member of a religion. However, after interviewing many teenagers, Smith concluded that most teenagers today don't know or understand the basic tenets and values of their religion and don't particularly care. Smith writes, "In many adolescents' lives, religion occupies a quite weak and losing position," but those teens who are religious "are doing significantly better in life on a variety of important outcomes than are less religiously active teens."[7] Smith blames teens' parents for the lack of religious training in the home and for not providing good role models of religious devotion. Moreover, in homes disrupted by divorce, death, or an unrelated parent figure—trends we see in families in American today—teens are much less likely to express feelings of religious devotion and attend church. These data suggest that many will not easily avail themselves of church resources.

Can Schools Substitute for Family Capital?

As an educator myself, I admit that I have a bias toward formal education in the creation of human capital. Historically many young men learned their professional trade from their fathers or other family members, while young women learned how to manage a household at the feet of their mothers. As industrialization emerged in the nineteenth century and the nature of work began to change, jobs and careers began to be structured by businesses instead of families, and many of those new jobs required some type of specialized training.

Although companies provided on-the-job training for most workers, the formal school system was relied upon to provide companies with literate (to a degree) employees who, in many cases, had some specialized training that would help them add value to their employers. In today's world, few families have the ability to personally provide the training necessary to prepare family members to compete successfully in many occupations. Families in industries like farming, fishing, and mortuary science continue to train family members to work in the family business or in a traditional job with a history of family involvement. But today, much education is formal and obtained through schools operated by the government, churches, or private institutions.

Access to good schools with good teachers varies dramatically from country to country. Literacy is just one measure of school effectiveness. Across the world some countries report 100 percent literacy (e.g., Andorra, Finland, and North Korea). The United States population is 99 percent literate.[8] Poorer countries such as those in sub-Saharan Africa and Latin America have much lower literacy rates (in the 50 to 70 percent range) since their federal and local governments lack either the will or the resources to provide a good education for all their citizens. In countries wracked by war and instability such as Afghanistan, Niger, and South Sudan, the literacy rate hovers just under 30 percent.

In many countries, including the United States, there are disparities regarding opportunities to attend a quality school and receive a good education. High school graduation rates, typically used as an indicator of effective schooling in the United States, vary dramatically. For example, during the 2014–2015 school-year Iowa graduated 90.8 percent of its students and Texas 89 percent, but in Nevada the rate was only 71.3 percent, with the District of Columbia bringing up the rear at 68.5 percent.[9]

A family's income plays a large role in the kind of education its children can receive. In the United States, for example, the overall high school graduation rate was 83.2 percent in 2015, but for lower income students the graduation rate was only 76.1 percent.[10] This is a consistent pattern that we see across the world—the poor have less access to educational opportunities. Robert Putnam of Harvard University, in his book *Our Kids: The American Dream in Crisis*, describes the differences in school systems experienced by several families in different regions of the United States.[11] For example, consider a high school in Santa Ana, California, where gangs, fights, and drugs are the order of the day; and where students, who typically receive little family support, spend most of their time after school trying to find enough food to eat and a safe place to stay rather than focusing on their homework. Conversely, in a high school located in an affluent neighborhood only a few miles away, the students are well cared for by their families, take advanced placement classes, and have high SAT scores; these students' major concerns are who to invite to the prom and what college to attend. Much of the income inequality in the United States (and around the world) is due to the fact that some families—who already have an abundance of human, social, and financial capital at their disposal—have the means to live in desirable areas and can send their kids to the best schools. However, those children whose families lack family capital are oftentimes left to fend for themselves in substandard schools where few go on to college and many end up in lower paying, minimum wage jobs. Thus, according to Putnam, the current dynamics affecting families and the economy in the United States are propelling the rich to get richer and the poor to get poorer. This is true worldwide; in 2016, sixty-two people had as much wealth as one-half of the people on our planet (3.5 billion), a smaller pool than in 2010, when 388 people controlled half of the earth's wealth.[12] Income inequality is clearly getting worse, not better, and access to quality education is one of the key factors affecting this trend.

Formal education, to the extent a person's family supports education and has access to quality schools, can strengthen family capital significantly. It provides skills needed to find employment, helps to strengthen social capital through associations made at school, and—since education is highly correlated with income—fuels personal and family financial capital. Furthermore, many schools have programs to help students with behavioral problems and some even have support groups for students who experience anxiety and depression. One of my grandchildren has benefited greatly from public school programs that help in dealing with autism. Thus, in addition to helping students prepare for a career, schools can also provide support for children with emotional and behavioral problems.

The difference in median household income (a good measure of family financial capital) in the United States varies greatly depending on level of education. The average household income in the United States was $58,044 in 2015. Table 8.1 shows household income broken down by education level.[13]

Table 8.1 Educational Attainment and Household Income in the United States—2015

Educational Level	Household Income
Less than 9th grade	$26,252
9th grade to 12th grade (no diploma)	$26,356
High School Graduate	$42,047
Some College (no degree)	$51,906
Associate's Degree	$62,485
Bachelor's Degree	$87,991
Master's Degree	$101,323
Professional Degree	$136,640
Doctorate	$121,244

The relationship between education and income is well known, and yet in the United States, many young people—particularly young men—are not taking advantage of educational opportunities that were afforded their parents. One recent report noted the following:

In the United States, [only] 30 percent of twenty-five to sixty-four-year-old non-students have attained a higher level of education than their parents. . . . only Austria, the Czech Republic, and Germany show a smaller percentage. By contrast, in

Finland, Korea, and the Russia Federation, 55 percent or more of adults who are no longer students have attained a higher level of education than their parents.[14]

Although several reasons likely explain this relative decline (one being the cost of higher education in the US), some studies point to the family as the primary culprit. A 2016 study by William Doherty and his colleagues showed that changes in family structure—particularly the increase in the past several decades of single parent households in the United States—have affected educational attainment among today's youths.[15] The authors of the study reported that increasing out of wedlock births and divorce rates have contributed to the following among children in these homes:

» Lower grades
» Lower standardized test scores
» Higher high school drop-out rates
» Reduced likelihood of attending college

These findings hold even when controlling for the socioeconomic status of the families involved. Family structure seems to have an especially strong impact on young men. When the father is absent from the home, young men are much less likely than young women to attend college. The researchers write, "The college enrollment gender gap . . . began to emerge about eighteen years after the beginning of major shifts in family structure. . . . The higher the non-marital birth rate grew, the lower the ratio of males to females [enrolled in college]."[16] When parents are not available to encourage education and academic achievement, children are less likely to see education as important in their own lives. And without a good education, young people in today's world will find it more difficult to contribute to the family capital that their own families will need in the future. Unfortunately, current dynamics in American families point to less encouragement of educational achievement.

Can Schools Provide Students with Character and Values?

The histories of most colleges and universities in the United States point to a connection to a religious tradition in their founding.[17] For example, the University of Chicago was initially funded by John D. Rockefeller as a Baptist school to encourage both secular learning and faith. The university saw itself as responsible to build character in its students and to provide them with the values and social tools necessary to lead a successful life. Over time, most religiously based schools, like the University of Chicago, have left their religious roots, and their curriculums and training have been driven by research and the scientific method. Secular knowledge, not character, is what counts. Although impressive advances in science have resulted, this trend appears to have left some college students bereft of values and beliefs that would serve them well. Because truth is currently a function of cultural relativism, few professors are willing to take a stand about what is right and wrong and what practices and values will lead to a better life. Thus, much to my chagrin as a college professor of over thirty years, I've seen a significant increase in binge drinking, sexual assaults, cheating, and plagiarism on American campuses. Most college students are left to figure out how to navigate life on their own or by getting advice from their friends, associates, and the media—and only at times from their parents, siblings, or other family members. When children grow up in unstable homes without instruction in important values and don't receive parental support, schools are often not equipped to serve as substitute parents to help students develop into well-rounded, empathetic, confident, and competent individuals. In 2016 I read a letter by a high school teacher named Steven Wedel, who teaches English in the Oklahoma City School District. Wedel was concerned that the Oklahoma state legislature and local voters weren't supporting schools like they should and that he needed both the support of the government and from his students' parents. Here are some excerpts from his poignant letter:

Open Letter to Oklahoma Voters and Lawmakers

Posted on February 26, 2016 by Steven E. Wedel

I am a teacher. I teach English at the high school of an independent district within Oklahoma City. I love my job. I love your kids. I call them my kids. I keep blankets in my room for when they're cold. I feed them peanut butter crackers, beef jerky, or Pop Tarts when . . . school breakfast or lunch isn't enough to fill their bellies. I comfort them when they cry and I praise them when they do well and always I try to make them believe that they are somebody with unlimited potential no matter what they go home to when they leave me.

What do they go home to? Sometimes when they get sick at school they can't go home because you and the person you're currently shacking up with are too stoned to figure out it's your phone ringing. Sometimes they go home to parents who don't notice them, and those are often the lucky kids. Sometimes they go home to sleep on the neighbor's back porch because your boyfriend kicked them out of the house and his dog is too mean to let them sleep on their own back porch. They go home to physical and verbal abuse. They go home looking for love and acceptance from the people who created them . . . and too often they don't find it. . . .

Often, they stay at school with me for an hour and a half after the bell rings because they don't want to go home to you. Reluctantly, they get on the two buses meant to take home students who stay for athletic practice, and they go away for a dark night in places I can't imagine.

Over 90 percent of the kids in my high school are on the free or reduced lunch programs. They walk hand-in-hand with Poverty and its brother Violence. They find comfort in the arms of your lover, Addiction. They make babies before they are old enough to vote. Or drive. And they continue the cycle you put them in. Sometimes I get through to a student and convince her that education is the way out of this spiral of poverty and despair. Then you slap them down for wanting to be better than you.

...Parents, I beg you to love your children the way we love your children.[18]

When our teachers' best efforts are undermined by what is happening in their students' homes and teachers aren't given sufficient resources, it's difficult to see how our school systems can be effective surrogates for family capital. When family capital is abundant in families, fewer school resources are needed to control student behavior, provide meals, and provide other types of support for the children. However, when family capital is lacking, school systems are often overburdened as they attempt to take over the role as the provider. This can create a vicious cycle. Unfortunately, families lacking family capital often live in school districts with fewer resources to help families nurture their children.

Can Out of Wedlock Births Be Reduced?

Given the negative emotional, behavioral, educational, and financial outcomes associated with out of wedlock births discussed in chapter 2, governments and schools have put a lot of energy into trying to reduce the number of children born to single mothers, with modest success. However, in the United States, the percentage of teen births to unmarried mothers rose from 29 percent in 1970 to 89 percent in 2014, despite a decline in out of wedlock births to teens since 2007.[19] This increase in births by unmarried teenagers has been fueled by the increased sexual activity of youth. One study reported the increase in sexual activity as teens get older: "30 percent of ninth graders reported having experienced sexual intercourse. The corresponding statistics for older teens were 41.4 percent for tenth graders, 54.1 percent for eleventh graders, and 64.1 percent for twelfth graders."[20] Sexual activity among the youth, as well as adults, has led to a proliferation of sexually transmitted diseases (STDs) in the United States. In 2016 there were 20

million new cases of STDs—the highest number in history—and about
one in three Americans, 110 million in all, have a sexually transmitted
disease according to the Centers for Disease Control (CDC). This costs
the US about $16 billion annually.[21]

Most of the programs to reduce out of wedlock pregnancies in the
US have been targeted at teens, since they are the most likely to have
children and not be married. Many of these young mothers drop out
of school and have to rely on family or government assistance, as few
receive child support from the child's father. This leads to a cycle of
poverty in such families, often continuing from one generation to the
next.

The George W. Bush administration promoted "abstinence sex
education" in schools, since refraining from sexual relations was the
only sure way to avoid an out of wedlock birth or a sexually transmitted disease and such education was morally acceptable to most of
Bush's constituents. Moreover, research has shown that virgins who
marry are more likely to have stable marriages than those who have
multiple sexual partners before marriage.[22] But these programs had little effect on sexual relations among teenagers since only 3 to 5 percent
of men and women currently report being virgins when they marry—
it was above 20 percent in the 1970s.[23]

One recent study describes some of the characteristics of sex education programs that have been effective in reducing out of wedlock
births:

> Many analysts and researchers agree that effective teen preg-
> nancy prevention programs (1) convince teens that not having
> sex or that using contraception consistently and carefully is the
> right thing to do; (2) last a sufficient length of time (i.e., more
> than a few weeks); (3) are operated by leaders who believe in
> their programs and who are adequately trained; (4) actively
> engage participants and personalize the program information;
> (5) address peer pressure issues; (6) teach communications
> skills; and (7) reflect the age, sexual experience, and culture of
> young persons in the program.[24]

This study also notes that counseling and educational programs for women who have had one child out of wedlock have been fairly successful in preventing future unwanted pregnancies by these women.

One teacher, Luis Miguel Bermudez from Colombia (which has the highest out of wedlock birth rate in the world), uses many of the seven principles just outlined in his high school sex education class in Bogotá.[25] Bermudez gives a no-nonsense class where he engages the students openly about sex, its consequences (including sexually transmitted diseases), abstinence, contraception, and how to handle relationships. He describes his results:

> It was common to see fourteen-year-old pregnant girls arriving to class and their education was practically over, and they were left with very few prospects. Some of the girls had two babies by sixteen, and I was worried about their futures. I said we should talk honestly and openly about sex. We needed a different approach. These kids aren't ignorant; they know a lot more about sex than we give them credit for! In 2011 we had roughly seventy pregnancies a year, and this year we have zero. We no longer have any pregnant students—not even one.[26]

Bermudez notes that he included boys in his pregnancy statistics to ensure accountability on the part of both the boys and girls. For his efforts, former Colombian President Juan Manuel Santos named Bermudez as the country's best teacher and praised his efforts to reduce teenage pregnancies.

Bermudez's example suggests that educational efforts can make a difference in out of wedlock birth rates, but such an approach requires considerable commitment on the part of teachers and schools. But more and more out of wedlock births are with older women not in school who probably won't be reached by such programs. Access to accurate information about the consequences of sexual relations plus access to contraceptives for those who choose to be sexually active are key to reducing out of wedlock births.

Reducing out of wedlock births is possible—though clearly not easy—for governments or other institutions interested in solving this problem.

NGOs as a Substitute for Family Capital

One may consider nongovernmental organizations (NGOs) as providing a substitute for family capital. The term was created by the United Nations Charter in 1945 through Article 71, which defines an NGO as independent from government and not-for-profit. In my role as academic director of the Ballard Center for Economic Self-Reliance located in the Marriott School of Business, I often interact with leaders of a variety of NGOs whose primary goal is to help lift people out of poverty. Roughly ten million NGOs exist throughout the world, according to an estimate.[27] They largely function through donations from private individuals or foundations and address a wide variety of issues—including health, education, violence, human trafficking, and financial security. I cannot cover all of the many aspects of NGOs here, but I will give a few examples of how they can provide human, social, and financial capital.

In terms of human capital, NGOs have been able to improve the health of their clients by eradicating diseases such as smallpox and polio through immunization programs. Programs to provide clean drinking water have had some success as have programs teaching basic hygiene and providing basic supplies to deal with first-aid or other minor medical problems. Other organizations (such as the Red Cross and Catholic Relief Services) provide aid during natural disasters such as hurricanes, earthquakes, or tsunamis or man-made disasters such as war—although such is not guaranteed.

NGOs also enhance human capital through education. NGOs often supplement formal education in countries where the government is unable to provide sufficient educational opportunities for their citizens. I often find myself working or researching with an NGO whose mission is to train the poor to start their own businesses, particularly in countries where jobs are difficult to come by.

An example of this type of NGO is the Academy for Creating Enterprise (ACE)—founded by Steve Gibson, a successful retired entrepreneur, and his wife Bette Gibson, an educator. (See chapter 4 for my earlier discussion about the group.) Initially started in the Philippines, the group expanded to other sites worldwide; from 2013 to 2015 I led a research team that looked at the impact of ACE training in Mexico City.[28] Besides basic entrepreneurial training, the NGO also provides continual mentoring through various follow-up seminars. Our study tracked ACE graduates from their three programs—residential training (eight weeks at the ACE academy), night classes, and classes taught in various regions of Mexico. We wanted to know if, after training, ACE graduates made more money and launched more successful businesses than a control group. The results were consistent with what we've seen in other studies on the impact of NGO education programs—there was some improvement in personal income and in business success (primarily measured by business growth), and a large percentage of ACE students were able to move out of poverty as a result of the ACE training.

Other NGOs try to help those in need by providing them with opportunities to develop social capital. The theory behind these types of NGO interventions is that most people in poverty lack mentoring and relationships that would help them succeed economically. While family connections are often the primary vehicle for garnering social capital, those without family support can turn to certain NGO programs as potential substitutes.

One United States NGO that purports to help individuals and families gain social capital is Circles.[29] Circles reaches out to those in poverty, and if an individual applies for the Circle program and is accepted, she becomes a Circle Leader. Circle Leaders meet twice a month with allies—one or more volunteers who provide the Circle Leader with access to social networks; emotional support; advice regarding complex issues; and help to set and achieve goals, though they do not provide any financial support. Circles also forms groups of community leaders who identify local barriers to moving out of poverty and create plans to help remove those barriers or help people overcome them. In their advertising literature, Circles quotes one Circle Leader named Trevor:

> [My allies] were friends and confidants who accepted my frustration with my situation and felt it with me. They allowed me to vent; made me laugh; held me accountable in kind, understanding ways; helped me work on interview skills; and above all else were there when things got rough. I probably wouldn't be where I am without them.[30]

Unfortunately, like most NGOs, Circles only reports anecdotal evidence that their program is effective.

The Becoming a Man (BAM) program based in Chicago likewise focuses on education and social support.[31] In 2016, 764 people were murdered in Chicago and over 3,000 were wounded in shootings, making the city one of the most dangerous places to live in the United States. The preponderance of perpetrators and victims of these shootings were young, African American males. The BAM program, started in 2001, enrolls students from grades seven to twelve in BAM training sessions in conjunction with their regular schooling. During the 2014–15 school year 2,185 students were served by 47 BAM counselors. In that year, BAM held 3,974 group sessions and 473 students received individual counseling.

The BAM program's thirty weekly group sessions focus on impulse control, emotional self-regulation, recognition of social cues, developing a sense of personal responsibility, and integrity. Most of the young men in the BAM program lack parental guidance and support—thus the BAM program and the counselors serve as role models to help provide direction for these youths. The results for these young men while in the program have been impressive:

» High school drop-out rates have been reduced to just 5 percent of BAM members.
» Violent crime arrests have lessened by 44 percent.
» Weapons crime and vandalism has gone down by 36 percent.
» Graduation rates have risen significantly.

Whereas some of these impressive results might be due to self-selection (i.e., those youths most amenable to change sign up for the BAM program), the BAM program provides a reasonable model for how to deal with the challenging problem of community violence. What happens to these young men when they graduate from the BAM program? Some evidence suggests that without continual support, these young men will go back to their traditional patterns of behavior—gang affiliation and gang violence—and the BAM program will not have had a lasting impact. In contrast, family support is generally for a lifetime and hence has a long-lasting impact.

Microcredit NGOs have played a significant role for many poor people by providing them with financial capital. Although some banks also provide this service, NGOs have had a greater impact. The microcredit movement, founded by Nobel Peace Prize winner Muhammad Yunus, has emerged as a major force in the world, serving millions of individuals—most of which would not have access to capital without microcredit. Professor Yunus saw that many of the poor in Bangladesh had good business ideas and were willing to work, but they had to either obtain money from loan sharks who charged exorbitant interest rates or go without. Thus, he started the Grameen Bank, which focused on giving small loans to poor people with entrepreneurial ambitions. Interest rates on microcredit loans are not cheap (most are over 30 percent annually) but they are clearly better than the alternatives.

Most of these loans are given to start a small business or finance an existing one. A recent survey of microcredit institutions revealed the following:[32]

» 111.7 million low-income clients held microcredit loans.
» Microcredit loans totaled $87.1 billion worldwide.
» NGOs serve 27 percent of global borrowers.
» India (39.5 million) and Bangladesh (21.8 million) had the most borrowers.

Some evidence suggests that microcredit has had a positive impact in the lives of many borrowers; however, uncertainty exists as to whether these NGOs are sustainable over the long-term without a significant infusion of donor funds. Some studies have indicated that when borrowers have clear objectives for the funds, two-thirds saw their situation improve or maintained, but much of the success of microcredit has to do with the initial situation of the borrower (current employment, income, education, and motivation).[33] Given that many individuals and foundations are willing to support microcredit NGOs and that banks are supporting many borrowers, it's unlikely that the services provided by these institutions will disappear any time soon; however, they may not be as reliable as the family in providing financial support and resources when needed.

Can Government Take Over the Role of Family?

The roles governments play in the lives of their citizens are tremendously diverse. For example, Scandinavian countries tend to take a cradle-to-grave approach to providing support for their citizens, while the poorer countries in Africa and Latin American have fewer resources and civil infrastructure to support their citizens in times of need. One country, Switzerland, had a referendum recently (that was defeated) to provide all its citizens a guaranteed income. If such a government program were in place, family financial capital, while still important, might not be needed as often to support family members.

In countries across the world, numerous programs provide individuals and families with important resources (mostly financial). For example, in the United States 21.3 percent of the population (about 52 million people) participate in a government assistance program each month.[34] While the percentage relying on government support varies largely depending on how the economy performs, it has tended to increase over time with only 18.6 percent of the population requiring assistance in 2009 (as the great recession was starting).[35] The US government also provides medical services to those who qualify for Medicaid or Medicare, preschool resources through Head Start and other programs, and free school lunches for those who qualify, along with certain after-school programs. Government also plays the major role in funding for schools as well as job training.

One of the more important government agencies in the United States that provides support for starting and growing businesses is the Small Business Administration (SBA).

Many of my clients have used SBA loans to benefit their businesses; the SBA loan portfolio totaled $124,118,505 in 2016.[36] Moreover, I have seen budding entrepreneurs take advantage of the SBA's training and mentoring programs that have improved their ability to succeed in business. And in some communities, small business incubators (largely funded by the government) provide small business owners with office space and other basic infrastructure to help them launch and grow their businesses. While the United States is one of the leading countries in the world providing these types of services to entrepreneurs, other countries recognize the importance of providing human, social, and financial capital to potential entrepreneurs and provide these resources to help them.

Governments can, and many do, provide resources to help develop a family's human capital and potentially encourage the development of new enterprises by family members.

Government Encouragement of Marriage and Child-Bearing

In AD 9 the Romans introduced a law known as *Lex Papia Poppaea* that imposed financial penalties on those who were not married after a certain age. In general, that law achieved its goal. However today, various government actions to encourage marriage—particularly among the poor—have generally been ineffective. For example, in the United States the George W. Bush administration created the Building Strong Families and Supporting Healthy Marriage initiatives to encourage people to marry and stay married. In evaluating these efforts, Robert Putnam concludes, "Despite isolated hopeful signs, however, neither of these experiments offered much evidence that

even well-designed, well-funded public programs can increase marriage rates or keep parents together. . . . I see no clear path to reviving
marriage rates among poor Americans."[37]

While government, churches, and other institutions can encourage marriage and stable relationships, the current narrative about
marriage dissuades today's young people from marrying. Some lower-
income, never-married adults cite "financial instability" as the major
reason they are not married. However, my research on family capital
indicates that marriage can help to solve that problem, as a married
couple pools their resources. It's an odd paradox that those who are
poor are rejecting a path that could lead them out of poverty.

Even though overpopulation is an issue in much of the developing
world, a declining population is a major concern for many industrialized nations. Nations with declining birth rates will eventually need
more workers to grow their economies and to provide taxes to care for
an aging population. But like those attempts to encourage marriage,
government programs have been relatively unsuccessful in motiving
citizens to have more children.[38]

In Sweden, a country with great state-run day care and maternity
leave, births are still well below replacement rate. In Russia, they have
tried almost everything to increase their birth rates. September 12,
2007 was designated by the Russian government to be Family Contact
Day when workers were given time off to procreate "for Russia." Nine
months later, those women who had babies on Russia Day won prizes
ranging from televisions to an SUV; this was called the "Give Birth to
a Patriot" incentive. Russia also instituted a program to pay women
$10,000 for having a second child. The Singapore government pays
mothers $9,000 for a second child and $18,000 for a third. The government also matches dollar-for-dollar savings accounts to pay for a
child's expenses and offers generous maternity leave. To combat its
declining birth rate, Korea has instituted similar programs that have
cost over $70 billion dollars over the past decade. But despite these
programs, Russia is still below replacement rate, Singapore's birth
rate continues to be one of the lowest in the world (.79), and Korean

birth rates are at historic lows. Results are similar in other developed countries. If current trends hold—and that's difficult to predict—the world's population will grow only because of high birth rates in Africa. Other continents will see declining or flat populations by the year 2100.[39]

Efforts to Strengthen Marriage Relationships

Strengthening your marriage will also strengthen your capacity for family capital. Various programs, government and otherwise, to strengthen marriage and cohabiting relationships have been more successful than those designed to encourage people to get married and have children. Professor Alan Hawkins, an expert on marriage education, has researched extensively on marriage preparation education, relationship development education, education for parents of blended families, and programs to help couples become successful parents.[40] Hawkins points out that marriage preparation programs are often required by certain religions, such as Catholicism. Such training, usually in a group format, includes discussions about expectations in marriage, problem-solving skills, and finances. Participants receive feedback on relationship strengths and weaknesses by filling out various personality inventories. Nine states in the United States have passed legislation encouraging couples to attend such programs, and those who do get a modest reduction in the cost of their marriage license. Hawkins notes that only about 37 percent of couples who marry go through such training, but the results of this education are impressive. A meta-analysis of thirteen studies on marriage preparation education reported the following:

> Of the thirteen most rigorous studies, twelve found that couples who participated in premarital education programs had significantly higher relationship skills and marital quality after the program compared to couples who did not participate. The researchers found that the average person who participated

in the premarital prevention program was better off after the program than 79 percent of the control-group couples who did not receive premarital education.[41]

Three primary reasons for premarital education success exist:

» It slows down the courting process and helps couples think more carefully about their decision to get married and the quality of their match—they get a more realistic preview of married life.
» It reinforces the idea that marriage is hard work and its success depends on skills, knowledge, and commitment.
» It alerts the couple to those resources available to help them in their marriage. Couples who have gone through premarital education are more likely to seek out counseling when they face difficulties in their marriage.

Another meta-analysis of fifty studies of such programs showed that premarital education programs improved the couples' communications skills but not necessarily their level of marital satisfaction.[42] Given the human, social, and financial costs associated with divorce and the break-up of families, Hawkins sees premarital education as a cost-effective way to strengthen families. Moreover, the results from several other studies point out that relationships and marital quality are enhanced when couples go through such training.[43]

But what about education for those who cohabit? Hawkins notes that about two-thirds of eighteen-year-olds believe that living together is a good way to test whether a marriage will succeed (which is untrue, as discussed in chapter 2).[44] Since more than two-thirds of couples live together before getting married, they should also be a target audience for premarital education even if they decide not to marry. Hawkins concludes, "I think couples who are living together (the majority) as well as those who are not (the minority) can benefit from formal preparation for marriage."[45]

Relationship development programs, as distinct from marriage preparation programs, help individuals assess the quality of their relationships, make wise choices about the future, and learn skills for a successful relationship. Remarriage education programs assist couples who are remarrying and want to avoid another divorce and learn how to live in a blended family. Marriage maintenance education is considered a check-up for married couples. Participants assess how they are doing in marriage and family living. The programs focus on clarifying family expectations and helping couples work through problems. Overall, all these programs have positive, albeit modest, results. Some more targeted programs focus on the poor, certain racial and ethnic groups, and couples in distress. Similarly, these programs appear to strengthen marriages, but the results are not strong. One potential bias in such studies is that people who seek out these programs are more motivated to change and thus benefit from the program. Clearly more work needs to be done to see what types of programs for married couples are cost effective, but current programs provide hope for those who want to succeed in marriage or maintain a long-term relationship.

When one partner files for divorce, particularly when children are involved, many states require some type of co-parenting education and training to mitigate some problems associated with divorce and to ensure both parties understand divorce ramifications. Hawkins has estimated that the direct and indirect costs of a single divorce in the United States (e.g., the costs of drug abuse, incarceration, drop-out rates, etc. associated with divorce) are approximately $18,000; thus any effort to reduce divorce by government is likely to be cost effective.[46] A book by Hawkins and his colleagues called *Should I Try to Work It Out?* presents research findings and options for those contemplating divorce; it is used by certain states to help educate couples on the consequences of divorce.[47] On a personal note, several years ago in an ecclesiastical role I counseled many couples considering divorce. That type of counseling is difficult and emotionally draining, since the conflict between partners is real and painful and the stakes are high. I made Hawkins's book required reading, and the couples generally found it to be very helpful—both the couples who stayed together and those who ultimately divorced.

Relying on Other Sources of Capital: The Problem of Unintended Consequences

In examining the role that churches, schools, NGOs, and government can play in providing support for families, you should be aware of the unintended consequences of using these nonfamily resources. Does assistance from nonfamily institutions enhance or undermine family capital, and if so, how? To explore this question I'll use the example of growth in welfare services in the United States since 1964 and its impact on families. One argument often made is that the War on Poverty, initiated by President Lyndon Johnson in 1964, actually created incentives for young, generally less educated women to have children out of wedlock in order to collect welfare benefits and remain dependent on the government—thus undermining family capital. Although I doubt someone would go through the pain, discomfort, and sleepless nights of pregnancy and childbirth just to get government assistance, it may be rational for a young woman to have a child if she has little hope in landing a good job and also wants someone (a baby) who loves her unconditionally. Moreover, the sexual revolution and general upheaval of the 1960s made having children out of wedlock less taboo and likely had an impact on the trajectory of out of wedlock births. In any event, the out of wedlock birth rate has grown from 7 percent in 1964 to over 40 percent by 2017, an increase of almost 600 percent.[48] One scholar on this topic described the situation this way:

> The burgeoning welfare state has promoted single parenthood in two ways. First, means-tested welfare programs . . . financially enable single parenthood. It is difficult for single mothers with a high school degree or less to support children without the aid of another parent. Means-tested welfare programs substantially reduce this difficulty by providing extensive support to single parents. Welfare thereby reduces the financial need for marriage. Since the beginning of the War on Poverty, less-educated mothers have increasingly become married to the welfare state and to the US taxpayer

rather than to the fathers of their children. As means-tested benefits expanded, welfare began to serve as a substitute for a husband in the home, and low-income marriage began to disappear. As husband left the home, the need for more welfare to support single mothers increased. The War on Poverty created a destructive feedback loop: Welfare promoted the decline of marriage which generated a need for more welfare. Second . . . the means-tested welfare system actively penalizes low-income parents who do marry. . . . If a low-income single mother marries an employed father, her welfare benefits will generally be substantially reduced. The mother can maximize welfare by remaining unmarried and keeping the father "off the books."[49]

The article's author—Robert Rector, a senior research fellow—argues that the government should reduce marriage penalties and replace them with incentives for single mothers and their children's fathers to marry. Government programs can certainly help families acquire capital to support the family, but they can also create unintended consequences that can undermine family capital.

Relying on resources and services outside the family can be risky since they can be eliminated when changes occur in the government or funding becomes unavailable. Family relations and support tend to be more enduring than those of these external entities; thus not developing or maintaining family capital or relying on external sources for support is probably unwise. Of course, when family support is unavailable the safety net provided by these institutions may be the only option.

Families must also be careful to not create unhealthy dependency with their support or enable family members engaging in destructive behaviors. The goal of the family should be to provide its members with family capital that allows them to be self-reliant and independent and eventually acquire resources that they can share.

31. "Youth Guidance: Guiding Kids to Bright Futures," BAM, https://www.wilsoncenter.org/
    sites/default/files/a.j._watson_presentation.pdf.

32. *Microfinance Barometer 2016* prepared by Oikocredit, http://www.convergences.org/
    wp-content/uploads/2016/09/BMF-EN-FINAL-2016-Version-web.pdf.

33. Ibid.

34. "21.3 Percent of U.S. Population Participates in Government Assistance Programs Each
    Month," *United States Census Bureau,* May 28, 2015 (Release # CB15-97).

35. *Welfare Statistics* prepared by the Statistic Brain Research Institute, http://www.statistic-
    brain.com/welfare-statistics.

36. *FY 2016 Agency Financial Report* prepared by the U.S. Small Business Administration,
    https://www.sba.gov/about-sba/sba-performance/performance-budget-finances/
    agency-financial-reports/fy-2016-agency-financial-report-afr.

37. Putman, *Our Kids: The American Dream in Crisis,* 244–45.

38. Jonathan V. Last, "Make Boomsa for the Motherland!," *Slate,* April 25, 2013, http://www.
    slate.com/articles/life/family/2013/04/can_a_country_boost_its_low_birth_rate_examples_
    from_around_the_world.html.

39. Tariq Khokhar, "The Future of the World's Population in 4 Charts," *The World Bank,*
    August 5, 2015, https://blogs.worldbank.org/opendata/future-world-s-population-4-charts.

40. Alan J. Hawkins, "Does It Work? Effectiveness Research on Relationship and Marriage
    Education," in *Evidence-Based Approaches to Relationship and Marriage Education* , ed.
    James Ponzetti (New York: Routledge, 2015), 60–73.
        Alan J. Hawkins, "Will Legislation to Encourage Premarital Education Strengthen
    Marriage and Reduce Divorce?" *Journal of Law & Family Studies 9 no.*1 (2007): 79–99.
        Alan J. Hawkins, *The Forever Initiative: A Feasible Public Policy Agenda to Help Couples
    Form and Sustain Healthy Marriages and Relationships* (North Charleston, South Carolina:
    CreateSpace Independent Publishing Platform, 2013).

41. Hawkins, "Will Legislation to Encourage Premarital Education Strengthen Marriage and
    Reduce Divorce?," 11.

42. Elizabeth Fawcett et al., "Do Premarital Education Programs Really Work? A Meta-
    Analytic Study," *Family Relations* 59 no. 2 (2010): 232–39.

43. Hawkins, "Does It Work? Effectiveness Research on Relationship and Marriage Education."

44. Ibid.

45. Hawkins, *The Forever Initiative: A Feasible Public Policy Agenda to Help Couples Form and
    Sustain Healthy Marriages and Relationships,* 150.

46. Hawkins, "Will Legislation to Encourage Premarital Education Strengthen Marriage and
    Reduce Divorce?"

47. Alan J. Hawkins, Tamara A. Fackrell, and Steven M. Harris, *Should I Try to Work It
    Out?: A Guidebook for Individuals and Couples at the Crossroads of Divorce,* (CreateSpace
    Independent Publishing Platform, 2013).

48. Robert Rector, "How Welfare Undermines Marriage and What to Do About It," *The
    Heritage Foundation,* November 17, 2014.

49. Ibid., 4.

You go through life wondering what is it all about, but at the end of the day, it's all about family.

Rod Stewart, singer

CHAPTER 9

BECOMING A RESOURCE-RICH FAMILY

The human, social, and financial resources of a family can fuel a business launch and provide an emotional, social, and financial safety net for family members in need, as I have argued throughout this book. A composite case study in this final chapter will crystallize what I've discussed in previous chapters concerning what individuals and families can do to have a resource-rich family.

What Individuals Can Do to Create and Preserve Family Capital: The Case of John and Martha

I thought about using a real case study of a family that had done everything right in developing and transferring family capital. Unfortunately, such a family doesn't exist (at least I don't think so). All families make mistakes and neglect some of the principles regarding family capital I have highlighted. So instead I created a composite case study gleaned from several families I have known or studied who provide good examples of what can be done to create and preserve family capital.

John and Martha Before Marriage

John and Martha grew up in the same small town in the midwestern United States and were introduced by John's cousin. They dated for eight months before they were engaged and had a five-month engagement before getting married. They had dated others before, but tended to have meaningful relationships—"hooking up" was not part of their dating repertoire. So they had learned how to build a positive relationship with another person.

Both John and Martha brought family capital into the relationship. John, trained as an engineer, had a good paying job, and Martha had an accounting degree and worked for a local accounting firm. When they married, John had $5,000 in savings and a small sedan and Martha had $10,000. Both had good relationships with their parents and siblings and also had developed good relationships with extended family. John and Martha regularly kept in touch with their family members via phone, email, Instagram and Facebook, so they knew what was happening in their family member's lives. Before marriage, the two did not cohabit, but they did discuss issues like finances, family roles, and whether or not to have children. They also received premarital counseling from their local clergyman.

Early in Marriage

Early in their marriage, John and Martha decided to implement the following customs in their family:

- » A date night each week
- » A few family parties each year for family members living in the area
- » The adoption of several traditions from each other's family, which provided them with an important link to the past

» Regular church attendance, along with projects at the local soup kitchen to help those in need
» Membership in two social clubs to expand their social network

Both agreed to be open and honest with one another and to avoid infidelity. In terms of open communication, Martha and John had an incident that helped them remember its importance. Martha told the following story:

> We once had a visitor to our home named Harry. The first morning he was visiting I burned the breakfast toast by accident. But Harry quickly said: "Martha, I really like burned toast—so don't worry about it." Thereafter, I decided to burn the toast a little bit each morning to accommodate Harry. However, after about three days of preparing Harry his burned toast he finally said, "Martha, what's with the burned toast? I'm tired of burned toast." To which I replied, "But I thought you liked burned toast." Harry confessed, "I only said that to make you feel better. I really hate burned toast." After that, I didn't burn the toast any more, but John and I used that incident to help us in our marriage. When either of us thought the other wasn't being truthful, one of us would say, "Remember Harry's toast."[1]

John and Martha pooled their finances and they were completely transparent with each other regarding their financial situation. They also had a budget and put 10 percent of their income into savings each month for emergencies and for retirement. Some conflicts arose in the marriage—John spent too much money, and Martha sometimes felt neglected by John—so John and Martha would periodically do a "start-stop-continue" activity for which they would sit together and discuss things they should start, stop, and continue to strengthen their marriage. They found this exercise to be very helpful. They also implemented Professor John Gottman's "5 to 1 ratio" in their marriage—five positive interactions between partners to one negative interaction.[2]

Such a ratio creates a reservoir of good will between partners along with stability in a marriage when times get tough. John and Martha were committed to making their marriage work.

After the Children Came

John and Martha had several children—they were surprised at how much attention children needed and how much work and money were involved in raising them. Still, their basic assumption was that the children were a gift and they had to do everything possible to nurture and support them so they would grow to be healthy and productive adults. Abuse, either physical or verbal, was not part of the family culture.

When the children were born, both John and Martha took paternity/maternity leave. Martha got eight weeks off and when she went back to work part-time, John took his paternity leave. Thus, for the first three months of life John and Martha exclusively cared for each child. After their leaves ended, Martha was fortunate to have her mother care for the children when she was at work. Martha eventually went back to work full-time once the children were in school, and John and Martha juggled their schedules as best they could to be present when the children left for school and when they came home. Soon, the couple decided to do the following:

» Create a family mission statement that described the family core values.
» Identify chores the parents and the children should do each week, which was put on a poster for all to see.
» Have dinner as a family each night.
» Create a will designating what should happen if one or both of them were to die.
» Acquire life insurance policies on John, Martha, and the children to protect the family against an untimely death.
» Read regularly to the children.
» Identify resources outside the family that could be used to help family members, while realizing that the family wouldn't want to be completely dependent on them.

» Allow the children to solve problems on their own—that is, be a mentor but not a helicopter parent.

As the Children Matured

As John and Martha's children matured, the couple went to great lengths to ensure their children would succeed in school: They helped with homework—John with reading and Martha with math. They took responsibility for their children's education, not assuming the school by itself would suffice. One parent always attended the children's parent-teacher conferences to check on their children's progress. They got remedial help from the teacher or other resources when children struggled.

Each day they set times to wake up, eat breakfast, do chores, practice musical instruments, do homework, play, have "screen time," and other such events. The schedule wasn't so rigid that changes couldn't be made, but the children had a clear understanding of what was expected of them each day. John and Martha believed such a schedule created stability for the children and allowed them to develop their talents and a sense of responsibility. Traditions such as camping, fishing, and visiting grandparents were established. The outdoor activities taught the children how to set up camp, cook food, stay warm and dry, and clean up before leaving camp. Family members were encouraged to attend each child's recital, ball game, play, or other such activities, schedule permitting. John and Martha would talk with their children individually about any problems, offering advice and encouragement. The family also began to have "family councils" where the family would get together to discuss family issues, listen to instruction of the parents, hear issues raised by the children, make decisions together, and just have fun.

The Teenage Years

As the children became teenagers, the parents began to share, in more detail, the family mission statement and values. The children helped articulate how those values could be expressed in their everyday lives.

The children were given opportunities to express their talents in different ways, and John and Martha got them involved in various service projects to help those in need.

The children would often talk to grandparents and extended family on the phone or by using FaceTime. The children were also encouraged by their parents to travel, be involved in extracurricular activities at school, and participate in other activities to develop their talents.

John and Martha started talking about careers to the kids when they were in their mid-teens. They were aware of a study by professors Brad Wilcox and Wendy Wang that points to a sequence of events that leads to financial stability and well-being for teenagers:[3] earn a high school diploma, get a job and start working full-time, and get married before having children (or don't have children if staying single). Of those who followed the three steps in order, only 3 percent were classified as poor. Even millennials from poor families and from different racial and ethnic backgrounds did better financially by following the "success sequence." However, 53 percent of millennials in the study who did not follow this sequence ended up in poverty.

Armed with this information, John and Martha encouraged their children to graduate from high school, get work experience during high school to prepare for a full-time job, and not engage in risky behaviors that would lead to an unwanted pregnancy. John and Martha had very frank discussions about sex with each child. The couple introduced the children to their friends who had careers they might be interested in. In a few instances, John arranged for his children to "job shadow" his friends. These family friends also became part of the children's broader social network.

At this time, John and Martha attended periodic marriage enhancement meetings to improve their marriage. They also attended marriage counseling when a particularly difficult issue arose that they weren't able to solve themselves—John's spending problem was getting worse. Marriage counseling proved to be very helpful to both of them.

After the Children Leave and Grandchildren Arrive

In their later years, John and Martha maintain regular contact with their children—now adults—and grandchildren. They continue to counsel their offspring regarding challenges and let them know what family capital might be available. The couple holds yearly family councils with their adult children and their spouses to give advice, review the basic elements of their will, and discuss what will happen with their assets when they pass away. They regularly send messages of encouragement and support to their sons, daughters, and grandchildren through email and other media, as they embrace their role as cheerleaders.

John and Martha organize family reunions, where they share the family mission statement and discuss favorite "war stories" about the family that exemplify the family's values. When possible, John and Martha visit their offspring and grandchildren and go on vacations with them as well as attend special occasions.

The couple has taken up genealogy as a hobby, and they gave each of their children a chart showing their family tree. John recently got a DNA test that he shared with the family. Martha and John also have written personal histories in which they share major events in their lives and have digitized and sent all family photos to the family. They want their progeny to know their rich heritage.

With good counsel from their lawyer and estate planner, John and Martha have revised their will to leave some inheritance to their grandchildren. They have also helped some family members financially when in need, with the approach of giving money rather than loaning it. Martha says, "I keep my purse open and my mouth shut." But Martha acknowledges that she doesn't want her family to feel entitled. So money just to help with schooling or the down payment on a house or car seems appropriate to her.

John and Martha have also constructed a family capital genogram to identify where family capital resides in the family and to think about how that capital might be used to benefit family members. John and Martha still talk with their sons and daughters about their careers (and at times with sons- and daughters-in-law) and give them advice

ABOUT FAMILIUS

Familius is a global trade publishing company that publishes books and other content to help families be happy. We believe that the family is the fundamental unit of society and that happy families are the foundation of a happy life. We recognize that every family looks different, and we passionately believe in helping all families find greater joy. To that end, we publish books for children and adults that invite families to live the Familius Nine Habits of Happy Family Life: *love together, play together, learn together, work together, talk together, heal together, read together, eat together,* and *laugh together.* Founded in 2012, Familius is located in Sanger, California.

Connect

> » Website: www.familius.com
> » Facebook: www.facebook.com/paterfamilius
> » Twitter: @familiustalk, @paterfamilius1
> » Pinterest: www.pinterest.com/familius
> » Instagram: @familiustalk

FAMILIUS

The most important work you ever do will be within the walls of your own home.

CPSIA information can be obtained
at www.ICGtesting.com
Printed in the USA
FSHW020734110619
58931FS

9 781641 701402